Step by Step

Microsoft® Windows® Me

Millennium Edition

PUBLISHED BY
Microsoft Press
A Division of Microsoft Corporation
One Microsoft Way
Redmond, Washington 98052-6399

Library of Congress Cataloging-in-Publication Data
Microsoft Windows Millenium Edition Step by Step / Catapult
       p. cm.
   Includes index.
   ISBN 0-7356-0990-X
   1. Microsoft Windows (Computer file) 2. Operating systems (Computers) I. Catapult, Inc.

   QA76.76.063 M524212 2000
   005.4'469--dc21   00-031889

Printed and bound in the United States of America.

3 4 5 6 7 8 9   QWTQWT   5 4 3 2 1 0

Distributed in Canada by Penguin Books Canada Limited.

A CIP catalogue record for this book is available from the British Library.

Microsoft Press books are available through booksellers and distributors worldwide. For further information about international editions, contact your local Microsoft Corporation office or contact Microsoft Press International directly at fax (425) 936-7329. Visit our Web site at mspress.microsoft.com. Send comments to *mspinput@microsoft.com*.

Intel is a registered trademark of Intel Corporation. Kodak is a registered trademark of Eastman Kodak Company. Microsoft, MSN, Outlook, Visio, WebTV, and Windows are either registered trademarks or trademarks of Microsoft Corporation in the United States and/or other countries. Other product and company names mentioned herein may be trademarks of their respective owners.

Unless otherwise noted, the example companies, organizations, products, people, and events depicted herein are fictitious. No association with any real company, organization, product, person, or event is intended or should be inferred.

For Catapult, Inc.
Managing Editor: Ellen Cornillon
Project Editor: Sarah J. Rogers
Production Manager: Sue Prettyman
Principal Compositor: Paul Vautier
Production/Layout: Kim McGhee,
   Pennie McGhee, Kathy Yoshikami
Writer: Mark Simpson
Copy Editor/Proofreader: Pamela Fassett
Technical Editor: Jacquelyn Orvis
Indexer: Julie Kawabata

For Microsoft Press
Acquisitions Editor: Susanne Forderer and
   Kong Cheung
Project Editor: Kim Fryer
Cover Illustration and Design: Patrick Lanfear

Contents

*Quick*Look Guide

Discovering what's new on
the Windows desktop,
see Lesson 1, page 4

Using the Folders list to move
and copy files and folders,
see Lesson 1, page 26

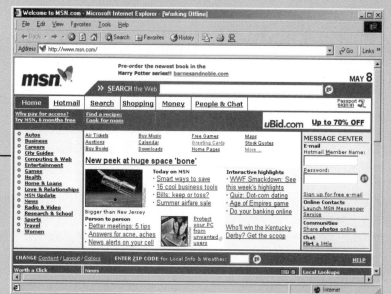

Using Internet Explorer 5.5
to connect to the Internet,
see Lesson 2, page 42

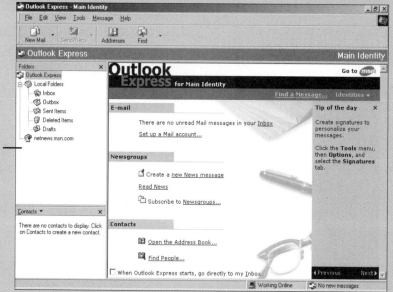

Setting up Outlook Express 5.5,
see Lesson 2, page 56

Setting up a direct cable
connection between
two computers,
see Lesson 3, page 75

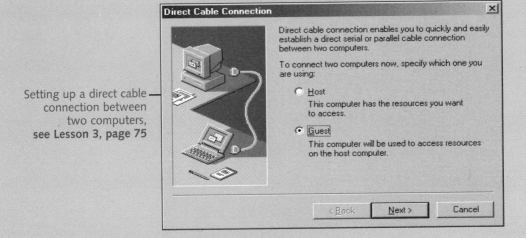

Setting up a
home network,
see Lesson 3, page 81

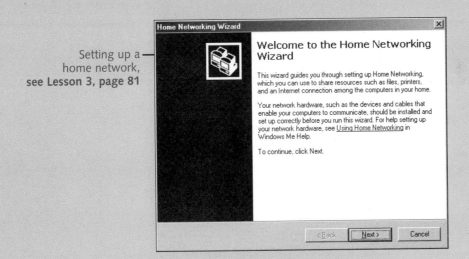

Using Phone Dialer to automate telephone tasks, **see Lesson 4, page 110**

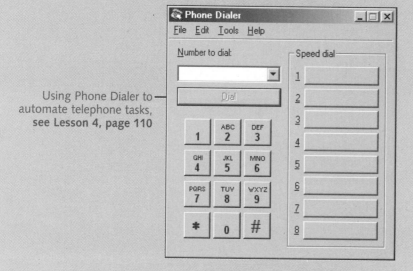

Setting up and calibrating game controllers, **see Lesson 4, page 124**

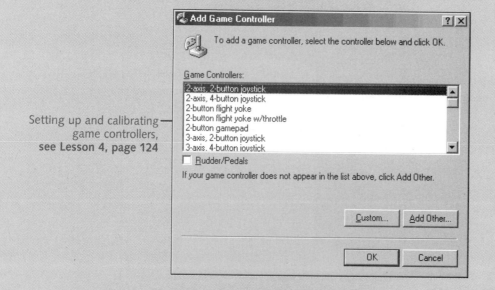

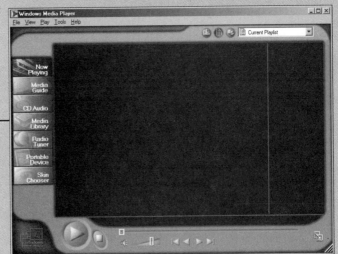

Using Media Player to play
and view multimedia files
from the Web,
see Lesson 5, page 141

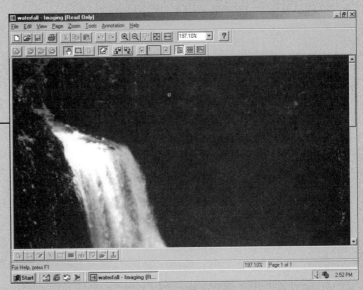

Editing photos taken
with a digital camera,
see Lesson 5, page 156

Downloading the latest
Windows Me updates,
see Lesson 6, page 184

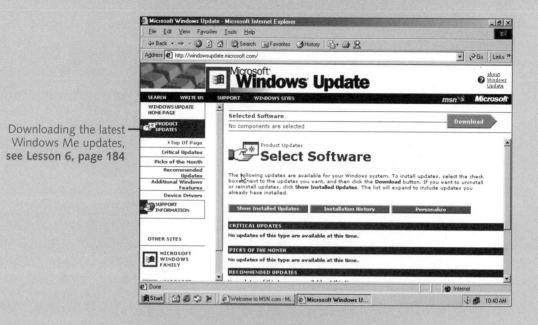

Scheduling maintenance tasks
to run automatically,
see Lesson 6, page 197

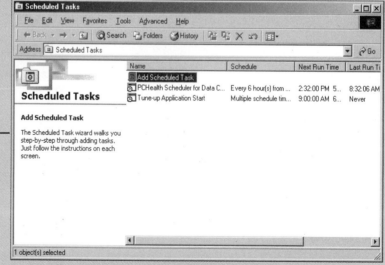

Backing up and restoring
files and folders,
see Lesson 7, page 208

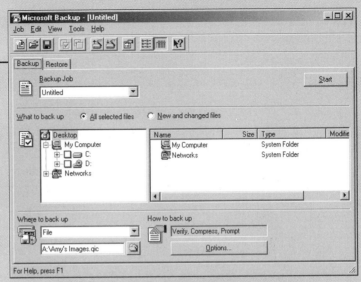

Setting up printers and sharing
printers on a home network,
see Lesson 7, page 216

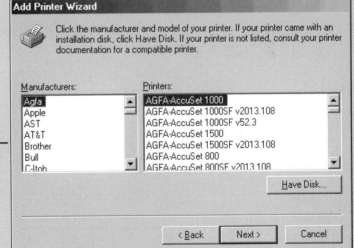

Finding Your Best Starting Point

Microsoft Windows Millennium Edition is the newest version of the Microsoft Windows operating system. Windows Me is designed specifically for home users, and includes much of the appearance and features of Microsoft Windows 98. However, Windows Me offers many new features and enhancements, including Microsoft Windows Explorer 5.5, easier home network setup, new gaming features, and a richer set of multimedia components. With *Microsoft Windows Me Step by Step*, you will quickly and easily learn how to use Windows Me.

Finding Your Best Starting Point in This Book

This book is organized for readers who have purchased a computer with the Microsoft Windows Millennium Edition operating system installed. If you are installing Windows Me yourself, read Appendix B, "Installing Microsoft Windows Me," before proceeding. Then, use the following table to find your best starting point in this book.

If you are	Follow these steps
New to computers, Windows, or graphical (as opposed to text-only) computer programs	1 Install the practice files as described in "Using the Microsoft Windows Me Step by Step CD-ROM." 2 Work through Lessons 1 through 7 chronologically.

If you are	Follow these steps
Upgrading	
from Windows 98 or Windows 95	**1** Learn about the new and enhanced features of Windows Me that are covered in this book by reading through the following section, "New Features in Windows Me."
	2 Install the practice files as described in "Using the Microsoft Windows Me Step by Step CD-ROM."
	3 Complete the lessons that cover the topics that interest you. You can use the Table of Contents and the *Quick*Look Guide to locate information about general topics. You can use the Index to find information about a specific topic or feature.

If you are	Follow these steps
Referencing	
this book after working through the lessons	**1** Use the Table of Contents to locate information about general topics, and use the Index to locate information about specific topics.
	2 Read the Quick Reference at the end of each lesson for a brief review of the major topics in the lesson. The Quick Reference topics are presented in the same order as they are presented in the lesson.
	3 Read the Review & Practice at the end of each part to review the topics in that part.

New Features in Windows Me

The following table lists the major new and enhanced features of Microsoft Windows Millennium Edition covered in this book and the lesson in which you can learn how to use each feature. You can also use the Index to find specific information about a feature or about a task that you want to perform.

The Millennium New icon appears in the margin throughout this book to indicate the features in Windows Me that are new or enhanced from Windows 98.

To learn about	See
Windows desktop	Lesson 1
Windows Help	Lesson 1
Personalized menus	Lesson 1
Customize This Folder Wizard	Lesson 1
Folder views	Lesson 1
Folders list	Lesson 1
Compressed folders	Lesson 1
Microsoft Internet Explorer 5.5	Lesson 2
Offline Web pages	Lesson 2
Microsoft Outlook Express 5.5	Lesson 2
Home Networking Wizard	Lesson 3
Internet Connection Sharing Wizard	Lesson 3
Game controller calibration	Lesson 4
Internet games	Lesson 4
Microsoft Windows Media Player	Lesson 5
DVD Player	Lesson 5
WebTV Program Guide	Lesson 5
Microsoft Movie Maker	Lesson 5
Automatic Windows Update	Lesson 6
System Restore	Lesson 6
Power management settings	Lesson 6

Corrections, Comments, and Help

Every effort has been made to ensure the accuracy of this book and the contents of the Microsoft Windows Me Step by Step CD-ROM. Microsoft Press provides corrections and additional content for its books through the World Wide Web at:

http://mspress.microsoft.com/support

If you have comments, questions, or ideas regarding this book or the CD-ROM, please send them to us.

Send e-mail to:

mspinput@microsoft.com

Or send postal mail to:

Microsoft Press

Attn: Step by Step Editor

One Microsoft Way

Redmond, WA 98052-6399

Please note that support for the Windows Me software product itself is not offered through the above addresses. For help using Windows Me, you can call Windows Me Technical Support at (425) 635-7031 on weekdays between 6 A.M. and 6 P.M., Pacific Time.

Visit Our World Wide Web Site

We invite you to visit the Microsoft Press World Wide Web site. You can visit us at the following locations:

http://mspress.microsoft.com

You'll find descriptions for all of our books, information about ordering titles, notices of special features and events, additional content for Microsoft Press books, and much more.

You can also find out the latest in software developments and news from Microsoft Corporation by visiting the following World Wide Web site:

http://microsoft.com/

We look forward to your visit on the Web!

Using the Microsoft Windows Me Step by Step CD-ROM

The CD-ROM inside the back cover of this book contains the practice files that you'll use as you perform the exercises in the book and multimedia files that demonstrate 8 of the exercises. By using the practice files, you won't waste time creating the samples used in the lessons—instead, you can concentrate on learning how to use Microsoft Windows Millennium Edition. With the files and the step-by-step instructions in the lessons, you'll also learn by doing, which is an easy and effective way to acquire and remember new skills.

important

Microsoft Windows Millennium Edition is not included with this book. Before you break the seal on the Microsoft Windows Me Step by Step CD-ROM package, be sure that this book matches your version of the software. This book is designed for use with Microsoft Windows Millennium Edition. To find out which version of Windows that you're running, you can check the product package or you can start the software. On the desktop, right-click the My Computer icon, and then click Properties. The version of your operating system will display in the General tab. If your product is not compatible with this book, a Step by Step book matching your software is probably available. Please visit our World Wide Web site at *mspress.microsoft.com* or call 1-800-MSPRESS (1-800-677-7377) for more information.

Hardware Requirements

To install and run Microsoft Windows Millennium Edition, your computer must have:

- A computer with at least a 150-MHz (megahertz) processor (also called a CPU). If you want to create movies with Microsoft Movie Maker, you will need a 300-MHz Pentium II processor or faster.
- At least 32 MB (megabytes) of RAM (memory). If you want to create movies with Movie Maker, you will need 64 MB of RAM.
- At least 480 MB of free space on your primary hard disk (the one that the operating system accesses each time you start your computer). You might need up to 635 MB of free hard disk space, depending on the options that you want to install. If you want to create movies with Movie Maker, you will need 2 GB of free hard disk space.
- A video adapter and a monitor that supports a resolution of VGA or better. (If you have purchased your monitor within the past six years, your monitor should meet this requirement.)
- A CD-ROM or DVD-ROM drive.
- A mouse (or other pointing device) and a keyboard.

To find out whether your computer meets these requirements, check the documentation that came with it or check with your technical support contact.

Additional Hardware to Use This Book

In addition to the computer itself, you will need 10 MB of free hard disk space to copy the practice files from the CD-ROM with this book and one or more of the following devices to perform one or more of the exercises. (Hardware requirements for completing lesson exercises are described at the beginning of each lesson.)

- A digital camera if you want to move graphics files to your hard disk.
- A game controller if you want to use one while playing games on your computer.
- A home network adapter (also called a network interface card, or NIC) and cable, or a home networking kit containing the necessary hardware for setting up a home network.

- A modem for connecting to the Internet and Dial-Up Networking.
- An Internet connection provided by an Internet service provider (ISP).
- A second computer running Microsoft Windows 95, Windows 98, or Microsoft Windows Millennium Edition that contains a network adapter.
- A high-speed direct parallel cable or a PC-to-PC file transfer serial cable suitable for connecting two computers.
- A sound card and speakers or earphones.
- A microphone if you want to record sound files.
- A TV tuner card (also called an adapter card) and a TV antenna or cable connection if you want to receive TV stations on your computer.
- Several formatted floppy disks.
- A music CD.

Installing the Practice Files

Follow these steps to copy the practice files to your computer's hard disk so that you can use them with the exercises in this book.

1 If your computer isn't on, turn it on now.

2 Remove the CD-ROM from the package inside the back cover of this book.

3 Insert the CD-ROM in the CD-ROM drive of your computer.

If a menu screen does not appear, double-click startCD.exe in the root of the CD-ROM.

4 Click the Install Practice Files option, and follow the prompts that appear on your screen.

5 When the files have been installed, remove the CD-ROM from your CD-ROM drive, and replace it in the package inside the back cover of the book.

If your computer is set up to connect to the Internet, you can double-click the Microsoft Press Welcome shortcut to visit the Microsoft Press Web site. You can also connect to this Web site directly at *mspress.microsoft.com*.

Using the Practice Files

Each lesson in this book explains when and how to use any practice files and folders for that lesson.

The practice files used in the lessons are as follows.

File or Folder Name	Description
Amy, Amy's Images, Charles, Chore List, Other Stuff, Personal Letters	Folders used in Lesson 1
Family Photos	Folder used in Lesson 3
Work Projects, Contacts	Folder and file used in Lesson 4
Movie, Annual Budget, Waterfall	Folder and files used in Lesson 5
Family Photos	Folder used in Lesson 7
Kid's Files, Chore List	Folders used in Review & Practice 1
Addresses, My Work	File and folder used in Review & Practice 2
Amy's Images	Folder used in Review & Practice 3

Using the Multimedia Files

Throughout this book, you will see icons for multimedia files for particular exercises. Follow these steps to play the multimedia files.

If a menu screen does not appear, double-click StartCD.exe in the root of the CD-ROM.

1   Insert the Microsoft Windows Me Step by Step CD-ROM in your CD-ROM drive.

2   Click the Browse CD option.

3   In the right pane, double-click the Multimedia folder.

    The Multimedia folder opens.

4   In the right pane, double-click the multimedia file that you want to view.

5   The video of the exercise plays.

6   Close Windows Explorer, and return to the exercise in the book.

Uninstalling the Practice Files

Use the following steps when you want to delete the practice files added to your hard disk by the Step by Step setup program.

1   Click the Start button, point to Settings, and then click Control Panel.

2   Double-click the Add/Remove Programs icon.

3   Click Windows Me SBS in the list, and then click Remove.

4   Click Yes when the confirmation message appears.

Need Help with the Practice Files?

Every effort has been made to ensure the accuracy of this book and the contents of the Microsoft Windows Me Step by Step CD-ROM. If you do run into a problem, Microsoft Press provides corrections and additional content for its books through the World Wide Web at

http://mspress.microsoft.com/support

Or send postal mail to:

Microsoft Press

Attn: Step by Step Editor

One Microsoft Way

Redmond, WA 98052-6399

Please note that support for the Windows Me software product itself is not offered through the above addresses. For help using Windows Me, you can call Windows Me Technical Support at (425) 635-7031 on weekdays between 6 A.M. and 6 P.M., Pacific time.

Conventions and Features in This Book

You can save time when you use this book by understanding, before you start the lessons, how instructions, keys to press, and so on are shown in the book. Please take a moment to read the following list, which points out helpful features of the book that you might want to use.

Conventions

Hands-on exercises for you to follow are given in numbered lists of steps (1, 2, and so on). A round bullet (●) indicates an exercise that has only one step.

- Text that you are to type and glossary terms that are defined at the end of the lesson appear in **bold**.
- The following icons identify certain types of exercise features.

Icon	Identifies
	Skills that are demonstrated in multimedia files available on the Microsoft Windows Me Step by Step CD-ROM.
MILLENNIUM New!	New features in Windows Me.

Other Features of This Book

- You can get a quick reminder of how to perform the tasks you learned by reading the Quick Reference at the end of each lesson.
- You can practice the major skills presented in the lessons by working through the Review & Practice section at the end of each part.
- You can see a multimedia demonstration of some of the exercises in the book by following the instructions in the "Using the Multimedia Files" procedure in the "Using the Microsoft Windows Me Step by Step CD-ROM" section of this book.

PART 1

Getting Started with Microsoft Windows Me

1

Customizing Windows for Personal Use

ESTIMATED
TIME
30 min.

After completing this lesson, you will be able to:

✔ *Recognize what's new on the Microsoft Windows Millennium Edition desktop.*

✔ *Customize the Start menu.*

✔ *Set up Windows for multiple users and add an additional user profile.*

✔ *Install and use accessibility features.*

✔ *Use the Magnifier to increase the level of magnification on the desktop.*

✔ *Change how folders look.*

✔ *Use the Folders list to organize folders.*

✔ *Compress folders to save disk space.*

✔ *Search for files.*

As you work through the exercises in this book, imagine that you are the parent of two middle school children. You work in the admissions office of a community college, and your spouse is a department manager for a local retail firm. Your family owns a computer that runs Microsoft Windows 98; the computer is used by all family members for a variety of tasks, ranging from games to homework to work that you and your spouse bring home from the office. You have just purchased a second computer with Microsoft Windows Millennium Edition

(Windows Me) already installed. Because there is some competition for computer time in your home, you plan to use both computers. First, however, you want to learn about the new features in Windows Me and get it set up for the whole family.

In this lesson, you will explore the Windows Me desktop to see what's new. You will also learn how to customize Windows, and then set it up so that family members can create their own personal desktops. You want to set up a **profile** for your son, who has motion disabilities, to make it easier for him to use the keyboard and mouse. You also want to know how Windows can be set up for your mother, who will be visiting you, and whose low vision makes it difficult for her to see objects on the computer screen. You also want to customize your folders and **compress** large folders to create more disk space. Finally, you want to explore the Search feature to locate lost files.

Practice files for the lesson

For additional information on copying practice files, see the "Using the Microsoft Windows Me Step by Step CD-ROM" section at the beginning of this book.

To complete the exercises in the lesson, you will need to use the Windows Me SBS folder and the following folders and the files they contain: Amy, Amy's Images, Charles, Chore List, Other Stuff, and Personal Letters. Before you can work with any of these exercise folders, you must copy them from the Microsoft Windows Me Step by Step CD-ROM to your hard disk.

Discovering What's New on the Windows Desktop

MILLENNIUM New!

The Microsoft Windows Millennium Edition desktop is similar to the Microsoft Windows 98 desktop. The consistency between the versions makes it easy to upgrade to Windows Me and quickly learn its new features.

Although the Windows Me desktop will look familiar, several items have been enhanced or added to make the desktop easier to use. The following list previews new items on the Windows Me desktop.

Icon	What's New
	Now contains the My Music, My Pictures, and the My Videos folders and **links** to My Network Places and My Computer.
	Now contains **shortcuts** to local drives and **Control Panel** only, plus links to My Documents, My Network Places, and Dial-Up Networking.
	Replaces Network Neighborhood. Simplifies viewing local networks and adding access to network locations. Contains icons to Add Network Place, the Home Networking **Wizard**, and links to other network and Internet resources.
	Microsoft Internet Explorer, version 5.5.
	Shortcut to Microsoft Outlook Express, version 5.5.
	Shortcut to Windows Media Player.
	Shortcut to Internet Connection Wizard for setting up an Internet connection. You can only use this shortcut once; when you attempt a connection, it disappears from the desktop.

important

This book assumes that Windows Me has been installed with the Typical setup. If any of the components discussed in this book do not appear in your installation of Windows Me, you will need to install them.

For more information on installing additional Windows components, see Appendix B, "Installing Microsoft Windows Me."

Windows Me is already installed on your new computer, which you have just set up. You want to take a quick look at Windows to see what's new on the desktop. In this exercise, you explore shortcuts on the Windows desktop.

1   Turn on your computer to start Windows Me.

Windows starts, and the Windows desktop appears.

Desktop icons
and shortcuts

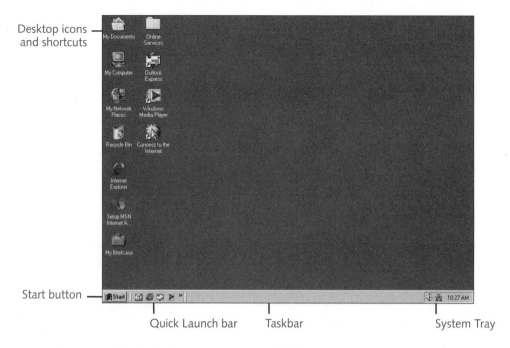

Start button

Quick Launch bar   Taskbar   System Tray

2   Double-click the My Documents folder.

The My Documents folder opens, displaying the My Music, My Pictures, and the My Videos folders, and links to My Network Places and My Computer.

3   Double-click the My Pictures folder.

The My Pictures folder opens, displaying several graphics files and links to additional Windows features.

tip

You can set up a screen saver that uses graphics stored in the My Pictures folder to create a slideshow, for example, a screen saver that shows family photographs. First, make sure that the graphics you want to use are located in the My Pictures folder. Then, right-click the Windows desktop, click Properties, and then click the Screen Saver tab. Click My Pictures Screensaver in the Screen Saver list.

4   Click the Sample graphics file.

A graphics thumbnail appears in the folder.

Close

5   Click the Close button, and then double-click the My Computer icon.

My Computer opens, containing icons representing the computer's drives and Control Panel, as well as links to other folders in the information pane on the left side of the folder.

6   Click the Close button.

Using Windows Help

New!

As in Microsoft Windows 98, the Help system in Microsoft Windows Millennium Edition is the primary source of information on how to use the program. Windows Me Help has been redesigned to include an easier, Web-like interface. In Windows Help, you can either type a word or phrase to search for or browse the index by topic.

The Windows Help topics include links to features in Windows so that you can quickly and easily complete a task without searching for the right tool. For example, the topic for setting up new hardware includes a link to the Add New Hardware Wizard.

Exploring Windows Help

1   Click the Start button, and then click Help.

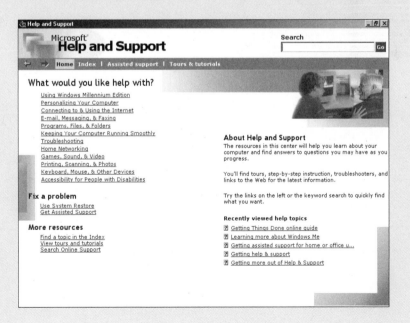

(continued)

continued

2   In the Search box, type **what's new** and then click Go.

3   Click the What's New In Windows Me topic.

4   Click Back twice to return to the Main Help screen.

Using Windows Troubleshooters

You can use Windows Troubleshooter to diagnose and fix network problems, printer problems, and modem problems, to name a few. Troubleshooter leads you step by step through a list of possible causes and solutions to help you identify the specific problem that you are having and how to fix it.

1   Make sure that Help is open.

2   In the What Would You Like Help With? list, click Troubleshooting, and then click a category in the Troubleshooting list.

Using Windows Online Help

Windows Me Help also includes links to help resources on the World Wide Web. You can find answers to specific problems as well as introductory and advanced information on using Windows. In Windows Help, you can locate the following resources.

- Getting Things Done Online: An online guide to additional information about how to use Windows Me. To find Getting Things Done Online, in the Help home page, search for Help, and then click the Getting Things Done Online Guide topic.

- Ask Maxwell: An online question and answer forum. You ask Maxwell a question, and he will provide answers. To find Ask Maxwell on the Help home page, click Search Online Support under the More Resources heading.

- Assisted Support: Links to other Web resources, such as the MSN Computing Central Forum. To find Assisted Support, on the Help home page, click Get Assisted Support under the Fix A Problem heading.

- Personal Online Support: a Web site offering links to additional resources, such as Microsoft Knowledge Base, which is a collection of technical information about Microsoft products, including Windows Me; Technical Support phone numbers; and requests for online support from Microsoft technicians. To find the Personal Online Support Web page, search for Help, click the Getting Help And Support topic, and then click the Personal Online Support link.

Customizing the Start Menu

The Start menu is the location from which you start most Microsoft Windows programs, and in Microsoft Windows Millennium Edition, the menu has been redesigned for easier use. The Start menu contains Personalized Menus, which are designed to hide items that you haven't used recently, making it easier to find frequently used menu items. You can also easily change Start menu settings; for example, by selecting or clearing a check box, you can view or hide commands to change the appearance of the Start menu. In addition, you can add, delete, and rename folders and program shortcuts on the Start menu. Finally, you can set up programs to start automatically by adding them to the StartUp menu.

For information on using the Address Book, see Lesson 4, "Using Windows for Work and Play."

In this exercise, you want to further personalize Windows and decide to customize the Start menu. First, however, you want to look at the Personalized Menus to understand how they work. Then, you decide to temporarily turn off the Personalized Menus until you become familiar with the contents of the Start menu. Next, you want to move the Address Book to a more accessible place on your Start menu for easier access.

> ### important
>
> By default, Personalized Menus are turned on but don't appear until you have used Windows Me long enough for Windows to determine which menu items you frequently use. If Personalized Menus do not appear, click the Start button, point to Settings, click Taskbar And Start Start Menu, and then make sure that the Use Personalized Menus check box is selected. If the check box is selected and Personalized Menus still do not appear, you cannot complete steps 1 through 5 of this exercise at this time. You will have to continue using Windows Me until Personalized Menus appear.

Unfold

1   Click the Start button, point to Programs, and then click the Unfold button at the bottom of the Programs menu.

   The menu expands to include less frequently used items.

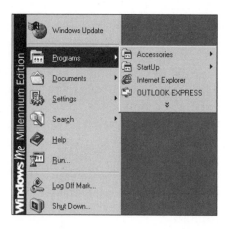

When Personal-
ized Menus first
appear, a mes-
sage is displayed
that explains
how to view
programs that
you have not
recently viewed.

2   Click the desktop to close the Start menu. Click the Start button, point to Programs, point to Accessories, and then click the Unfold button on the bottom of the Accessories submenu.

The submenu expands to include less frequently used items.

tip

If Personalized Menus are turned on and you move the pointer over a collapsed menu, the menu expands after a few seconds.

You can also
open the
Taskbar And
Start Menu
Properties dia-
log box from
Control Panel.

3   Point to Settings, and then click Taskbar And Start Menu.

The Taskbar And Start Menu Properties dialog box appears.

4   On the General tab, clear the Use Personalized Menus check box, and then click OK.

5   Click the Start button, point to Programs, and then point to Accessories.

The entire submenu appears.

6   Right-click and drag the Address Book to the blank area under the Windows Update command on the Start menu.

A shortcut menu appears.

tip

As you position the pointer under the Windows Update command, a horizontal I-beam pointer appears on the menu to indicate where the object will be placed when you release the mouse button. If a circle with a line through it appears, move the mouse pointer just slightly until the I-beam pointer appears.

7   On the shortcut menu, click Copy Here.

The Address Book is copied from the Accessories submenu to the Start menu.

8   Click the desktop to close the Start menu.

Setting Up Windows for Multiple Users and Creating Additional User Profiles

You expect that your entire family will want to use the new family computer, but you don't want your children or your spouse to change your desktop settings. In Microsoft Windows Millennium Edition, you can set up user profiles, which are a collection of settings that affect the desktop display, desktop folders, the Start menu, and e-mail. For example, you can set up a user profile for yourself that includes the settings for your personalized desktop, and then create a password for your desktop. Other users who log on to Windows will not be able to modify your settings—unless, of course, they log on with your name and password.

Profiles, however, do not prevent others from accessing files and folders. Files and folders can still be found in Windows Explorer or by using the Search option.

When you set up a user profile, Windows treats the existing configuration as the default. For example, if you have already set up a desktop theme before setting up a user profile, that desktop theme becomes the default desktop display setting. As you set up the user profiles, you can elect to change parts of the default settings (such as the changes you have made to the Start menu) or keep them the same.

In this exercise, you decide to set up a profile for yourself so that other family members cannot change your desktop settings, and then you set up a profile for your son who will want to apply a clever color scheme to his desktop display.

For a demonstration of how to set up Windows for multiple users, in the Multimedia folder on the Microsoft Windows Me Step by Step CD-ROM, double-click MultipleUsers.

1   Click the Start button, point to Settings, and then click Control Panel to display the contents of the Control Panel folder.

2   Click the View All Control Panel Options link, and then double-click the Users icon to start the Enable Multi-User Settings Wizard.

3   Click Next.

The Add User dialog box appears.

4   Type your name, and then click Next.

Each user profile will be identified by name.

5   In the Password box, type a password, press Tab, and then type the password again.

You do not have to use a password, but it is a good idea if you have anyone in the household that you want to block from either using or changing your desktop settings.

6   Click Next.

The Personalized Items Settings dialog box appears. You can select items to personalize in the new profile.

For more infor-   **7**   Click Create Copies Of The Current Items And Their Contents.
mation on Per-
sonalized Items   You do not select the check boxes in the Items area because you want to
settings, see   retain the current settings for the items, such as the current desktop settings
"Understanding   and the Start menu settings.
the Personalized
Items Settings   **8**   Click Next, and then click Finish.
Options" later
in this section.   The wizard creates your user profile. A message prompting you to restart
                          your computer is displayed. The new profile will not take effect until you
                          restart your computer.

9   Click Yes.

Windows quits, your computer restarts, and then the Enter Password dialog box appears, displaying your name.

tip

To delete a user profile, in Control Panel, double-click the Users icon, select the user, and then click Delete.

important

You can create an additional user profile from Control Panel. However, because you have already set up a user profile, the Enable Multi-User Settings Wizard does not appear again when you double-click the Users icon. Instead, you add additional user profiles directly from the User Settings dialog box.

10 In the Enter Password dialog box, type your password, and then click OK to display the Windows desktop.

11 Click the Start button, point to Settings, and then click Control Panel to display the contents of the Control Panel folder.

You may need to scroll down or maximize the screen to see the Users icon.

12 Double-click the Users icon.

The User Settings dialog box appears, displaying the user profile you just set up.

13 Click New User, click Next, type **James** and then click Next.

14 In the Password box, type **JKA** and press Tab. Type **JKA** again.

15 Click Next.

The Personalized Items Settings dialog box appears.

16 In the Items area, select the Start Menu check box.

The Start menu, which you modified in an earlier exercise, will be reset to Windows defaults so that your son can customize it.

17 Click Create Copies Of The Current Items And Their Contents, click Next, and then click Finish.

You remain logged on as yourself until you restart the computer or log off Windows from the Start menu.

18 Close the User Settings dialog box and Control Panel.

tip

To change your user profile password, make sure that you are logged on using your user profile. In Control Panel, double-click the Passwords icon, and then click Change Windows Password.

tip

To set up Windows so that a list of users is displayed when Windows starts, right-click My Network Places, and then click Properties. On the Configuration tab, click Add. In the Select Network Component Type dialog box, click Client, and then click Add. In the Manufacturers list on the left, click Microsoft. In the Network Clients list on the right, click Microsoft Family Logon, and then click OK. In the Primary Network Logon box, click Microsoft Family Logon, and then click OK. Click Yes when prompted to restart your computer.

Understanding the Personalized Items Settings Options

When you set up or change a profile, the options you select in the Personalized Items Settings dialog box will affect your new profile in various ways, depending on whether you choose to create copies of the current items or create new items. If you choose the Create Copies Of The Current Items And Their Contents option, the settings of any item you selected will be retained. For example, if you selected the Start Menu option, any programs that had been added to the Start menu will be retained in the new profile. However, if you selected the Create New Items To Save Disk Space option, programs that had been added to the Start menu will not be retained in the new profile.

The following table explains the effects of choosing items in the Items list and then selecting Create New Items To Save Disk Space.

For more information on Internet Explorer and Web pages, see Lesson 2, "Setting Up Internet Accounts and E-mail."

Item Selected	Effect
Desktop Folder And Documents Menu	File shortcuts currently included on the Start\Documents menu will not be included in the new profile.
Start Menu	Program shortcuts currently included on the Start\Programs menu will not be included in the new profile.
Favorites Folder	Shortcuts included on the Start\Favorites menu will not be accessible in the new profile. To add this folder to your Start menu, go to Start\Settings\Taskbar And Start Menu. Click the Advanced tab, and then select the Display Favorites check box.
Downloaded Web Pages	Downloaded Web pages will not be included in the new profile.
My Documents Folder	Files or folders in My Documents will not be accessible in the new profile.

Recovering from a Lost Password

If you ever forget your password, you can delete the password file and then set up a new password. When you create a password, it is stored in the Windows folder on your computer. The password file always has the extension .PWL, and the file name is the user profile name. For example, the password file for the Amy user profile would be named Amy.pwl.

1   On the desktop, double-click the My Computer icon, double-click the Local Disk icon, and then click the View The Entire Contents Of This Drive link.

2   Double-click the Windows folder, and then click the View The Entire Contents Of This Folder link.

3   Scroll through the list to locate the files with the .PWL extension. The files are listed in alphabetical order after the folders. The file name will be in the form username.pwl, where "username" is the name of the user profile.

4   Delete the .PWL file.

5   Start Windows using your user profile, and then type a new password in the Enter Password dialog box.

tip
You can also open Control Panel, double-click Users, select the name in the Users list, and then click Set Password. You can also change the Personalized Items Settings from the User Settings dialog box.

Configuring Windows for Accessibility Needs

You can set up Microsoft Windows Millennium Edition so that it is easier to use for people with special needs. You can make modifications to keyboard response, sounds, display elements, and the mouse from the Accessibility Properties dialog box in Control Panel. However, an easier method for setting up Windows for users with special needs is to use the Accessibility Wizard, which steps you through the process. In fact, the wizard suggests changes based on a particular need or disability that you specify. The wizard will configure Windows for vision, hearing, and mobility needs.

Your son has juvenile rheumatoid arthritis, which makes it difficult for him to use the keyboard and mouse. You want to set up Windows so that ordinary tasks, such as selecting objects and typing, are easier for him.

In this exercise, you aren't sure which accessibility changes should be made, so you decide to use the Accessibility Wizard to guide you through the process of making Windows easier to use for your son. First, you log on as your son, and then you start the Accessibility Wizard.

Your name will be included after the Log Off command (for example, Log Off Amy).

1   Click the Start button, click Log Off, and then click Yes.

The Enter Password dialog box appears.

2   Click James, press Tab, type **JKA** and then click OK.

You are now logged on as your son. The Accessibility options will affect his profile only.

3   Click the Start button, point to Programs, point to Accessories, point to Accessibility, and then click Accessibility Wizard.

The Accessibility Wizards starts.

Because you are setting up Windows for a user with a particular mobility need, you do not need to make changes to the screen font size.

4   Click Next.

The Text Size screen displays text samples in three font sizes. If you have a vision disability, you can change the text size in the wizard by clicking one of the text samples.

5   Click Next, clear the Change The Font Size check box, and then click Next.

6   On the Set Wizard Options screen, select the I Have Difficulty Using The Keyboard Or Mouse check box, and then click Next.

7   On the StickyKeys screen, click Yes, and then click Next.

The StickyKeys feature is turned on so that you do not have to press multiple keys simultaneously for multiple-key combinations like Ctrl+Alt+Delete.

8   On the BounceKeys screen, click Yes, and then click Next.

BounceKeys is turned on so that repeated keystrokes will be ignored.

9   On the BounceKeys Settings screen, click Next.

10   On the ToggleKeys screen, click Yes, and then click Next.

The ToggleKeys option is turned on so that a sound will play if the Caps LockSysRq, Num Lock, or Scroll Lock key is pressed.

11   On the Extra Keyboard Help screen, click Yes, and then click Next.

The Extra Keyboard Help option will offer ToolTips for keyboard shortcuts in programs that make them available.

12   On the MouseKeys screen, click Yes, and then click Next twice.

The MouseKeys option is turned on so that the keypad can be used to manipulate the mouse pointer.

13   On the Mouse Cursor screen, in the Black column, click the large mouse pointer, and then click Next twice.

The mouse pointer size and color are changed.

14   On the Mouse Speed screen, position the Mouse Pointer Speed slider so that it is half way between the middle setting and Slow, and then click Next four times.

StickyKeys

How quickly the mouse pointer moves across the screen is changed. The accessibility changes you selected are listed. You have set up the Accessibility options for the James user profile. Three icons are displayed on the System Tray, indicating that you have turned on StickyKeys, BounceKeys, and MouseKeys.

BounceKeys

15   Click Finish.

16   Press Ctrl, Alt, Delete in sequence.

MouseKeys

The Close Program dialog box appears. Because you have turned on the StickyKeys option, you do not have to press the keys simultaneously.

important

If you press two keys simultaneously, for example, Ctrl+Alt, StickyKeys is turned off until you log back on.

17   Click Cancel, and then press Num Lock twice.

MouseKeys Off

Your computer makes a sound because you have turned on the ToggleKeys option. The MouseKeys icon on the System Tray changes to indicate when it is toggled off.

18   Click the Start button, click Log Off James, and then click Yes.

19   In the Enter Password dialog box, click your name, press Tab, type your password, and then click OK.

tip

Windows Me also includes an on-screen keyboard that may be useful for mobility-impaired users. To open the on-screen keyboard, click the Start button, point to Programs, point to Accessories, point to Accessibility, and then click On-Screen Keyboard.

Using the Magnifier

You can use either the Accessibility Wizard to set up Microsoft Windows Millennium Edition for users who have low vision, or you can turn on the Magnifier. You can use the Accessibility Wizard to make several changes to how Windows displays objects and text, such as increasing the size of Windows controls and icons and making changes in color scheme and screen contrast. You can also use the Magnifier to make objects on the screen easier to see, and it can be easily turned on and off. For that reason, the Magnifier can be a good choice for a visually challenged user sharing your computer only on occasion.

Your mother's vision has declined to the point that she has difficulty seeing objects and text on the computer screen. She is coming to visit you and will want to use your computer to send e-mail messages. You want to set up Windows so that your mother can easily use it.

In this exercise, you want to set up your computer for your mother who will be using your computer only a few times during her visit. You decide that setting up the Magnifier is a better choice for her than stepping through the Accessibility Wizard.

1   Click the Start button, point to Programs, point to Accessories, point to Accessibility, and then click Magnifier.

The Windows screen is split horizontally. The top portion of the screen shows a magnified version of the desktop, which is visible at normal magnification in the lower half. The Magnifier Settings dialog box appears.

2   Click the Magnification Level up arrow once to increase the level of magnification to 3.

3   In the Presentation area, select the Start Minimized check box, and then click Exit.

The Magnifier Settings dialog box will be minimized the next time the Magnifier is turned on.

Adjusting Accessibility Settings

You can change the font size in Control Panel, which might be a good option for some users with special vision needs. In Control Panel, double-click the Display icon, and then click the Appearance tab. In the Scheme list, you can select the Windows Standard (Extra Large) or several other Large or Extra Large options. Or, you can change the font size of individual elements. In some Windows programs, you can zoom to magnify the display, and in Microsoft Internet Explorer, you can change the text size on the View menu. If you have special needs, you should experiment with the accessibility and display options to find the combination of settings that works best for you.

Instead of using the Accessibility Wizard to turn on accessibility options, you can set them up directly from the Accessibility Properties dialog box. You can also make adjustments to the accessibility options once you have used the wizard to set them up. You can turn on or make adjustments to the keyboard, sound, display, and mouse, plus other adjustments to how the accessibility features function on your computer.

To adjust other accessibility settings, in Control Panel, double-click the Accessibility Options icon, and then click a tab in the Accessibility Properties dialog box to change a specific setting. The following table describes changes you can make to the settings.

Area	Accessibility Feature	Function
Keyboard	StickyKeys	Allows one-key-at-a-time entry for key combinations like Ctrl+Alt+Delete.
	FilterKeys	Ignores brief, repeated keystrokes.
	ToggleKeys	Generates a sound when pressing Caps LockSysRq, Num Lock, or Scroll Lock.
	Show Extra Keyboard Help in Programs	Shows extra keyboard shortcuts in programs.
Sound	SoundSentry	Generates visual warnings when the system makes a sound.
	ShowSounds	Displays captions for sounds and speech.

Area	Accessibility Feature	Function
Display	High Contrast	Changes colors and fonts for easier reading.
	Cursor Settings	Changes the mouse pointer blink rate and mouse pointer width.
Mouse	MouseKeys	Enables the numeric keypad to control the mouse pointer.
General	Automatic Reset	Turns off accessibility features if Windows is idle for a selected period of time.
	Notification	Gives a warning when turning accessibility features on and off.
	SerialKey Devices	Sets up alternative input devices to replace the keyboard and mouse.

Customizing Folder Appearance

If you have used previous versions of Microsoft Windows, you have probably changed your desktop display by adding wallpaper, changing desktop color schemes, or creating other special effects. In much the same way that you can customize your desktop, you can also customize folders by adding templates, background images, colors, and comments about the folder contents. In fact, Microsoft Windows Millennium Edition includes an enhanced Customize This Folder Wizard, which steps you through the process of changing folder appearance.

When you customize a folder, you can apply one of several built-in **HTML** templates. Depending on the template, you can view more or less information about the files in the folder.

Folder Template	Description
Standard	Includes icons and file names; displays information about selected files. Standard is the default folder style.
Classic	Traditional Windows folder appearance. Includes icons only.
Simple	Similar to Classic style but includes file names along with the icons.
Image Preview	Used for viewing and organizing image files. Includes an image viewer and links to a scanner, camera, and slideshow for viewing folder images.

In addition to using templates, you can add a folder background color, pattern, or picture, and change the file name color and background. You can also include a comment to help identify the folder's contents.

In this exercise, you enhance the appearance of your folders so that they are functional yet pleasing to look at. You also decide to add a comment to a folder to help you identify its content at a later time.

1 On the desktop, double-click the My Computer icon.

2 Double-click the Local Disk icon, and then click the Maximize button.

Maximize

The contents of your Local Disk drive are displayed. A list of all folders and files on your hard disk as well as information about disk space, usage, and links to other desktop folders is displayed.

3 Double-click the Windows Me SBS folder, and then double-click the Amy's Images folder. You may have to scroll down to see it.

The folder opens, and icons representing the image files are displayed.

You can also right-click an empty space in the folder, and then click Customize This Folder.

4 Click View, and then click Customize This Folder to start the Customize This Folder Wizard.

5 Click Next.

The first wizard screen appears. By default, the Customize option is selected as well as the Choose Or Edit An HTML Template For This Folder check box.

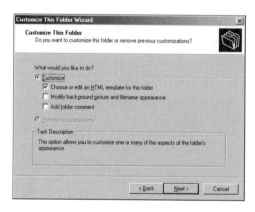

You cannot customize the Windows or Program Files folders.

6 Select the Modify Background Picture And Filename Appearance check box and the Add Folder Comment check box, and then click Next.

The Standard template in the Change Folder Template screen is selected by default. You can preview other templates by clicking them.

7   Click the Image Preview template, and then click Next.

Available background image file names are displayed.

8   In the Select A Background Picture From The List Below box, click Windows Millennium.jpg.

The image appears in the Preview box.

9   In the Filename Appearance area, click the Background button, choose yellow from the color palette, and then click OK.

The background behind the file names will be yellow.

10   Click Next, and then in the Folder Comment box, type **These are the images I like to use in family letters and cards.**

11   Click Next, and then click Finish.

The customized template and background are displayed.

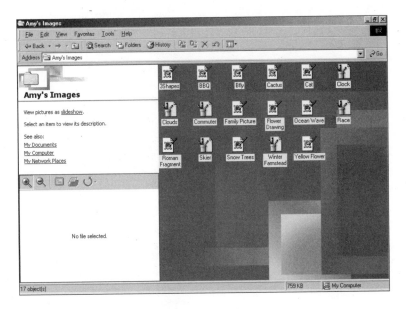

12   Click the Flower Drawing image file.

A preview of the image appears in the Image Viewer. Using the buttons on the Imaging Preview toolbar, you can zoom the image in and out, preview it full screen, print it, and rotate it.

tip

You can also right-click the Imaging Preview toolbar for additional Image Viewer selections. If you select the Zoom feature, click the image to activate it.

You can control the slideshow with the slideshow controls.

13   Click the View Pictures As Slideshow link to display the image.

14   Move the mouse to display the slideshow controls on the upper-right corner of the screen.

The controls are displayed. After a few seconds, the slideshow starts and displays each picture in the folder.

Close The Window

15   Click the Close The Window button to close Slideshow view.

16   On the Standard Buttons toolbar, click Back.

The contents of the Windows Me SBS folder are displayed. The Amy's Images folder is selected, and the folder comment is displayed in the Windows Me SBS information pane.

tip

To remove folder customization, start the Customize This Folder Wizard in the folder that you customized, click Next, and select Remove Customizations. Then, work through the wizard to remove the enhancements you do not want.

Viewing Information About Files and Folders

By default, the contents of Microsoft Windows Millennium Edition folders are presented in the Large Icon view. Windows Me also includes other views, each of which can be useful in particular situations. Although the folder view is often a matter of personal preference, choosing the best view can make navigating in and selecting from folders easier, depending on such variables as the number and type of files in the folder. You can easily switch among the views, but when you change a folder view, the view is changed for the active folder only. The following table suggests how you can use each view effectively.

Views

tip

To change views, on the Standard Buttons toolbar, click the Views button, and then click the view you want to use. Or, on the View menu, click a view.

Folder View	Use
Large Icons	Helps to quickly distinguish file types. Large icons are easier to see than smaller icons or text but do not include information about file properties, such as date created or file size. If a folder contains many files, it can be difficult to see all the files without having to move through them.
Small Icons	Helps to quickly distinguish file types but are more difficult to see than large icons. This view can be useful if the folder contains a large number of files.
List	Similar to Small Icons view but organizes icons in a list, which can be easier to move through if the folder contains a large number of files.
Details	Includes small icons and file names, plus file details such as file size, type, and date modified. Because the details are immediately visible, this view can be useful for quickly distinguishing among files by their date and size.
Thumbnails	Provides thumbnail views of image files. Useful for previewing images without having to open them or customize the folder.

Depending on the folder view you have chosen, you can view details about files and arrange the list of files:

■ To view details about a file, position the pointer over the file name or file icon.

■ To view details about a file in the folder pane, click the file. The details are displayed on the left side of the folder. (The folder options must be set to enable Web content in folders.)

■ To arrange icons, on the View menu, point to Arrange Icons, and then select the way you want your icons to be arranged.

Using the Folders List to Move and Copy Files and Folders

Microsoft Windows Millennium Edition has made dragging files between folders much easier, particularly when the folder you are moving an item to is located on another level in the folder hierarchy. For example, moving Amy's Images folder to the Amy folder is easy because both are visible in the Windows Me SBS folder. But moving the Amy's Images folder to My Documents would be difficult because that folder is not visible. In Windows Me, you can open the Folders list that contains all of the folders on your hard disk, which makes it easy to drag a selected folder to a folder on another level in the folder hierarchy.

You have started to organize your hard disk by creating folders for your family and yourself. In this exercise, you want to complete the job by moving several folders to a better location and then copying a file to another folder.

For a demonstration of how to use the Folders list to move and copy files and folders, in the Multimedia folder on the Microsoft Windows Me Step by Step CD-ROM, double-click FoldersList.

1   On the Standard Buttons toolbar, click Folders.

The Folders list is displayed. The list displays icons for all the folders on your hard disk, icons for other drives attached to your computer, and other folders on the desktop.

Folders list

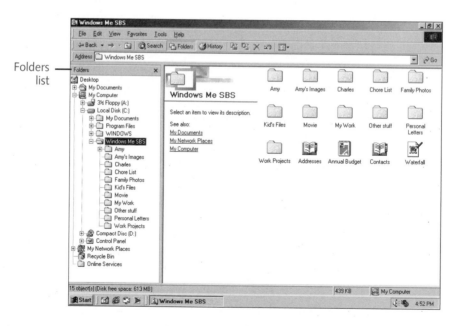

Customizing Windows

2   In the Windows Me SBS folder, click the Chore List folder, drag it to the My Documents folder, and then release the mouse button.

The folder is moved to the My Documents folder.

3   Click the plus sign (+) next to My Documents.

The Chore List folder is displayed in the My Documents folder.

4   In the right pane, double-click the Amy folder, and then double-click the Our Budget folder to open both folders.

5   Press and hold Ctrl, click the 2000 Expenses file, and drag it to the Charles folder in the Folders list.

The file is copied to the Charles folder.

6   On the Standard Buttons toolbar, click Back twice, and then double-click the Amy's Images folder to open it.

7   With the right mouse button, drag the Clouds file to the Personal Letters folder in the Folders list, and then release the mouse button.

A shortcut menu appears.

8   Click Copy Here to copy the file to the Personal Letters folder.

9   On the Standard Buttons toolbar, click the Up button twice.

The contents of the your Local Disk drive are displayed in the right pane of the folder.

10   On the Standard Buttons toolbar, click Folders to close the Folders list.

11   Double-click My Documents, and then click the Chore List folder.

12   On the Standard Buttons toolbar, click the Delete button, and then click Yes.

Up

Delete

tip

You can also use Windows Explorer to manage and organize files and folders on your hard disk. Windows Explorer is similar to the Folders list in that you can use Windows Explorer to view the contents of your computer as well as to move and copy files. In some cases, Windows Explorer might be more convenient because you can start it directly from the Start menu: right-click the Start button, and then click Explore.

Using Compressed Folders to Save Disk Space

When you compress a file, folder, or an entire disk, the contents take up less space. In fact, a file might take up less than half the space it takes in an uncompressed form. Using compression is useful in several situations. If you are using an older version of Microsoft Windows and you need extra space on your hard disk, you can use a compression **utility program** like Microsoft Drive Space to compress the entire hard disk, depending on how your drive is formatted. You can also compress an entire floppy disk, for example, when you want to copy a very large file to a floppy disk. More often, though, you'll want to compress a single file or folder, which you can do with special utility programs like Drive Space.

When you create a compressed folder in Windows Me, you can open the compressed folder on computers running older versions of Windows.

Microsoft Windows Millennium Edition includes a folder-compression utility that you can use to compress the contents of folders. Compressed folders are particularly useful in two situations: copying large files to floppy disks or sending large attachments in e-mail. If you often transfer files between computers—such as between your computer at home and your computer at work—you might discover that some of your files are too large to fit on a floppy disk. You can compress those files in Windows Me to reduce their size so that more data will fit on a single floppy disk.

If Compressed Folders does not appear on the Send To menu, you will need to install it. For help installing Windows components, see Appendix B, "Installing Microsoft Windows Me."

When you attach large files to an e-mail message, the time it takes to send and receive the e-mail message is increased, which is especially noticeable if you are using a slower modem and sending your e-mail messages over standard telephone lines. But if you compress the files before you attach them to your e-mail message, the sending and receiving time is decreased. In addition, some e-mail programs limit the size of files that you can attach, so sending a very large file can be impossible without compressing it first.

In this exercise, you want to send a family photograph file to your brother through e-mail. Because you want to send many files that are fairly large, you decide to compress the files before you send them and then view the contents of the compressed folder. You also want to create a compressed folder to hold several items that you want to transfer to your computer at work.

1   Make sure that the Windows Me SBS folder is open, and then right-click the Amy's Images folder, point to Send To, and then click Compressed Folder.

A compressed folder, also named Amy's Images, is created.

Compressed folders are identified
by the zipper design on the folder

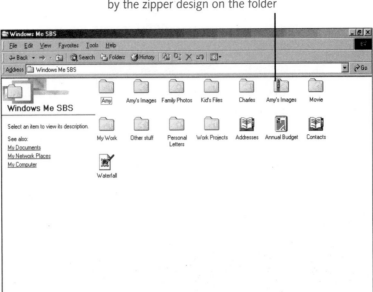

2   Right-click the original Amy's Images folder, and then click Properties.
The Amy's Images Properties dialog box appears.

*Your folder size
might be differ-
ent depending
on your com-
puter configu-
ration.*

Folder
size

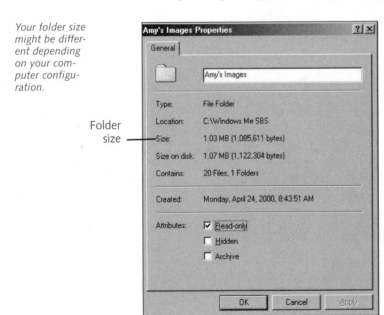

Customizing Windows

3   Click Cancel to close the dialog box.

4   Right-click the compressed Amy's Images folder, and then click Properties.

The size of the compressed Amy's Images folder is displayed.

5   Close the Amy's Images Properties dialog box.

You can open any file in a compressed folder the same way you open a noncompressed file.

6   Double-click the compressed Amy's Images folder.

The folder opens. It contains a copy of the Amy's Images folder.

7   Double-click the copy of the Amy's Images folder inside the compressed folder.

The folder opens, and the contents of the folder are displayed. The files are compressed versions of the original files in the Amy's Images folder.

8   Right-click the first image file, and then click Properties.

The Compressed Item Properties dialog box appears. The original and packed sizes of the file are displayed.

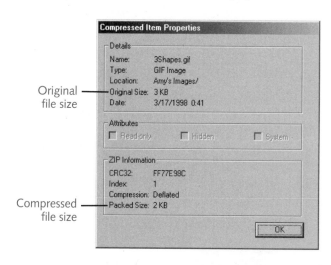

Original file size →

Compressed file size →

9   Click OK, and then in the Amy's Images folder, click the Close button to redisplay the contents of the Windows Me SBS folder.

Close

10 Right-click an empty space in the Windows Me SBS folder, point to New, and then click Compressed Folder.

A new compressed folder is created. The file name is selected.

11 Type **Take to the Office** and then press Enter to rename the new compressed folder.

12 Double-click the Amy's Images folder to display its contents.

You can compress a file by copying it to a compressed folder.

13   On the Edit menu, click Select All.

14   Right-click the selection, and then click Copy.

15   Click Back on the Standard Buttons toolbar to redisplay the contents of the Windows Me SBS folder.

16   Right-click the Take To The Office folder, and then click Paste.

The files are compressed as they are copied to the folder.

17   In the Windows Me SBS folder, click Close.

---

tip

You can decompress a file by dragging it from the compressed folder to a regular folder or to the desktop. You can decompress an entire folder by right-clicking the folder, and then clicking Extract All.

Using Search to Find Files

Once you have organized your folders in Microsoft Windows Millennium Edition, you will find it easier to locate your files. But as the number of files increase, it can be easy to forget where you put them, particularly files that were created a long time ago. Also, children who use the computer might not understand the file system and inadvertently save a file in a different directory without realizing it. Then, when they try to find the file, they might have trouble locating it.

If you can remember or guess at details about the file—a partial name, for instance, or the date it was created—you can usually locate the file quickly by using Search. When you use Search, you can look for files by specifying different criteria. You can search by name, or you can search by a word or phrase that a document contains. You can also search by the date the file was created, the file type, and the file size. Finally, you can specify where Windows searches—your entire hard disk or another drive, all subfolders on a drive, or a specific folder. The broader your search criteria, the longer it takes Windows to finish the search. Any information you can specify speeds up the process. For example, if you can remember that you created a file during a particular month, you can specify the month as one of your search criteria to speed up your search.

After you specify your search criteria and begin the search, the search results are displayed in the Search Results pane. You can preview and open files from the Search Results pane as well as move or copy them.

In this exercise, you want to find a letter you wrote to a friend. You don't remember the name of the letter and decide to search for it rather than open all of your letters to find the right one. Then, you offer to help your daughter, who created a picture of herself, saved it, but cannot locate it.

1   Click the Start button, point to Search, and then click For Files Or Folders.

The Search Results window opens.

Maximize

2   Click the Maximize button.

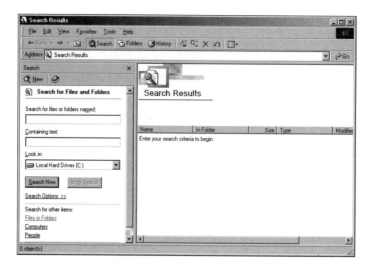

tip

You specify the search criteria in the Search pane on the left of the screen, and the results are displayed in the right pane. By default, Search will search for files or folders on your entire hard disk.

3   In the Containing Text box, type **Martha**

Martha is the name of the friend whose letter you want to find.

4   In the Look In list, click Browse.

The Browse For Folder dialog box appears.

5   Expand My Computer and Local Disk, and then click Windows Me SBS.

You know that the file is located somewhere in the Windows Me SBS folder. By specifying that folder, you will speed up your search because Windows will not look in other folders on your computer.

6   Click OK.

7   Click the Search Options link.

The Search Options box is displayed.

8   Select the Advanced Options check box.

The Search Subfolders check box and Case Sensitive check box are displayed. The Search Subfolders check box is selected. You are not sure in which folder within the Windows Me SBS folder the letter is located, and the Search Subfolders option will search all of the subfolders within that folder.

9   Click Search Now.

After a few seconds, the search results are displayed in the Search Results pane, and a file is displayed. You can open the file directly from the pane by double-clicking it.

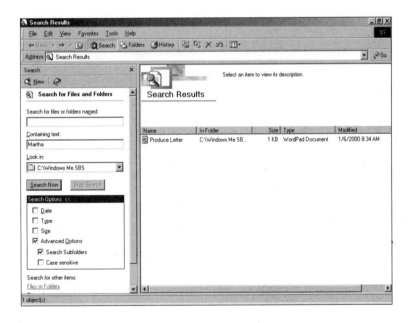

10   Click New in the Search pane.

The information from the previous Search Results pane is cleared.

11   In the Search For Files Or Folders Named box, type ***.bmp**

The file your daughter misplaced is a Microsoft Paint file, which can be identified by the .bmp extension. The asterisk (*) is a **wildcard** character that can be used as a substitute for any character or string of characters. The *.bmp means that Windows will search for all files ending with .bmp.

12   In the Search Options area, select the Date check box.

Several options are displayed following the Date selection. By selecting one of the date options, you can search for files modified, created, or accessed in a specified period in the past. You know that your daughter created the file during January 2000, so you can narrow the search by specifying a date or date range.

13   In the Date list, make sure that Files Modified is selected.

You will search for files created on a certain date or during a certain period.

14   Make sure that the Between And option is selected, and then click the Between arrow.

A calendar is displayed. The current date is circled in red.

15   Click the left Calendar arrow to locate December 1999, and then click December 31.

The date is entered in the first date box.

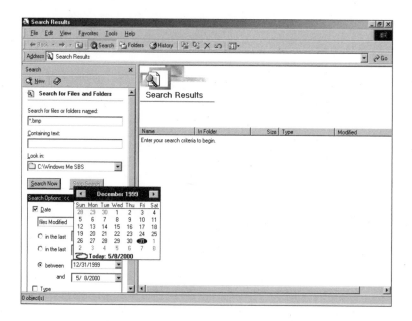

16 Click the And arrow, move to February 2000, and then click February 1.

The date is entered in the second date box. Windows will search for all .bmp files created on any date in January 2000.

17 Click Search Now.

Search locates the .bmp files created in January 2000, Shapes.bmp and Picture Of Me.bmp. Your daughter indicates that the Picture Of Me.bmp file is the one she is looking for.

tip
You can save the results of a search by clicking Save Search on the File menu.

Close

18 In the Search Results pane, click the Close button to display the Windows desktop.

Searching for People and Web Sites

Windows Search is not restricted to searching for files on your computer. You can use Search to locate people on the Internet or who are listed in an address book on your computer or on a network. You can also search for a Web site.

Locating someone in an address book

For information on using the Address Book, see Lesson 4, "Using Windows for Work and Play."

1 Click the Start button, point to Search, and then click People.

2 In the Look In box, click the address book in which you want to search.

3 On the People tab, you can type part of the person's information in the corresponding boxes; for example, the person's first or last name, the person's e-mail address, or the city where the person lives.

4 Click Find Now.

(continued)

continued

Locating someone on the Internet

important
You must first have an Internet connection set up on your computer and use an Internet directory service that specializes in finding e-mail addresses, phone numbers, and names.

1   Click the Start button, point to Search, and then click People.
2   In the Look In box, click a directory service, fill in the Name and E-Mail boxes, and then click Find Now, or click Web Site to view the directory service Web site.

Locating a Web site

For information on connecting to and using the Internet, see Lesson 2, "Setting Up Internet Accounts and E-mail."

important
You must first have an Internet connection set up on your computer.

1   Click the Start button, point to Search, and then click On The Internet.
2   In the Find A Web Page Containing box, type a search keyword and then click Search.

Lesson Wrap-Up

In Lesson 1, you previewed some of the new features on the Microsoft Windows Millennium Edition desktop, and you customized the Start menu to make program items easier to locate. You added user profiles to safeguard customized desktop settings and then set up accessibility options for users with special needs. Next, you customized the appearance of a folder and used the Folders list to move and copy files. Finally, you learned how to compress folders and search for misplaced files on your hard disk.

If you are continuing to the next lesson:

●   Close any open windows before continuing.

If you are not continuing to other lessons:

1　If you are finished using your computer for now, log off Windows.

2　If you will not be using your computer for a long time, shut down Windows.

Glossary

compress To reduce the size of a file or folder by using a file-compression utility.

Control Panel A utility used for controlling Microsoft Windows or hardware settings.

HTML Hypertext Markup Language. A language used for creating Web pages. In Windows, you can view HTML objects, such as templates or images, on your desktop and in folders.

link A graphic, word, or phrase in one location that points to another element in a different location. When you click a link, the element it points to is displayed. For example, when you click the My Computer link in My Documents, My Computer opens. Word and phrase links are often underlined and in a different color than surrounding text. You click the link once to go to the element the link is connected to.

profile A record of personal settings maintained by Windows for a particular user, such as a user's choice of desktop background color or Start menu settings. Also called a user profile.

shortcut An icon that is linked to a program, folder, file, or Web page. For example, when you double-click the Microsoft Outlook Express shortcut on the Windows desktop, Outlook Express starts.

utility program A program designed to accomplish a specific maintenance task, like compressing or backing up files.

wildcard A character, such as * or ?, that can be used to represent other characters. In the file name *.bmp, the * stands for any string of characters; in the file name Mar?.bmp, the ? stands for any single character.

wizard An interactive Help utility that guides you through a series of steps to accomplish a complex task. For example, the Enable Multi-User Settings Wizard steps you through the process of setting up a user profile.

Quick Reference

To customize the Start menu

1   Click the Start button, point to Settings, and then click Taskbar And Start Menu.

2   Click the options you want on the General tab.

To set up Windows for multiple users and create additional user profiles

1   Click the Start button, point to Settings, and then click Control Panel.

2   Double-click the Users icon.

3   Click New User, and then work through the wizard steps.

To configure Windows for accessibility needs

1   Click the Start button, point to Programs, point to Accessories, point to Accessibility, and then click Accessibility Wizard.

2   Follow the wizard steps.

To use the Magnifier

●   Click the Start button, point to Programs, point to Accessories, point to Accessibility, and then click Magnifier.

To customize folder appearance

1   Open the folder that you want to customize.

2   Click View, and then click Customize This Folder.

3   Work through the steps in the wizard.

To use the Folders list to move and copy files and folders

1   Open a folder containing files or folders, and then on the Standard Buttons toolbar, click Folders.

2   To move a folder or file, drag it to a folder in the Folders list.

3   To copy a folder or file to the Folders list, press and hold Ctrl, and then drag it to the Folders list.

To compress folders to save disk space

1   Right-click the folder you want to compress.

2   Point to Send To, and then click Compressed Folder.

To search for files

1   Click the Start button, point to Search, and click Files Or Folders.

2   Enter the search criteria, and then click Search Now.

2

Setting Up Internet Accounts and E-mail

ESTIMATED
TIME
30 min.

After completing this lesson, you will be able to:

✔ *Set up an Internet connection.*

✔ *Set up an Internet connection with Dial-Up Networking.*

✔ *Control the type of Internet content that your browser displays.*

✔ *Set up and update an offline Web page.*

✔ *Set up Microsoft Outlook Express to send and receive e-mail messages.*

✔ *Allow multiple users to send and receive e-mail messages with Outlook Express.*

✔ *Read messages in newsgroups with Outlook Express.*

Your family has experience browsing the Internet and exchanging e-mail messages and has discovered that using the Internet is one of the most educational things they can do with a computer. However, because you do not have an Internet connection at home, your family has only used the Internet and e-mail at work or school. You volunteer to set up both the Internet and e-mail accounts so that your family can access the Internet and send e-mail messages from home.

In this lesson, you will learn how to set up an Internet connection and use your browser to connect to the Internet. Next, you will identify a home page for your browser and Web content to display on your desktop. You will also set up your browser so that your children view only age-appropriate Web content. Then, you will set up Microsoft Outlook Express for multiple users and read messages from **newsgroups**.

Practice files
for the lesson
To complete the exercises in this lesson, you will need a modem set up (for example, dial-up or cable) and account information from an **Internet service provider** (ISP). If you have a slow Internet connection, the time it takes to finish this lesson may be longer than 30 minutes. No practice files are required to complete the exercises in this lesson.

> ## important
> The exercises in this lesson are based on Microsoft Internet Explorer version 5.5 because it is included with Microsoft Windows Millennium Edition. If you are using a different browser, the procedures will be similar, but some details might differ. Check your browser documentation for specific instructions.

Using the Internet Connection Wizard

For more information on ISPs, see "Setting Up MSN and Other National Internet Service Providers" later in this section.
When you sign up with an ISP, oftentimes the provider will walk you through the procedures of setting up the Internet connection with them. For example, when you sign up with MSN, by clicking the Setup MSN Internet Access icon on the desktop, the MSN Wizard leads you through the setup steps. However, if you change your computer configuration or need to set up a new computer with an Internet account that you already have, you might need to set up the connection yourself. Fortunately, Microsoft Windows Millennium Edition provides the Internet Connection Wizard to step you through setting up the connection. Before you run the wizard, however, you need to have the following information handy from your ISP:

- A telephone number to connect to your ISP.
- A password.
- A log-on name or user name.
- E-mail account information, such as the name of the server or servers you will use for sending and receiving e-mail messages.

You can also create a connection in Dial-Up Networking. See "Using Dial-Up Networking to Set Up Additional Online Connections" later in this lesson.
In this exercise, you have decided to sign up with a local ISP rather than a national online service. When you called the ISP, they provided you with connection settings, such as a telephone number to connect with, password, user name, and the name of the server you will connect to.

important

Your modem must be set up to complete this exercise. In most cases, new computers come with the modem already set up. If you are installing Windows Me over an older version of Windows, Windows will usually retain your modem settings so that you do not have to set up your modem again. If you need to, you can manually set up your modem or make adjustments to it in the Modems folder in Control Panel. Consult Windows Help or your modem documentation for more information.

If the Connect To The Internet shortcut is displayed on your desktop, you can also double-click it to start the Internet Connection Wizard.

1 Double-click the Microsoft Internet Explorer icon on the desktop.

The Internet Connection Wizard starts.

important

The Internet Connection Wizard is started the first time you start Microsoft Internet Explorer 5.5. If you have already started Internet Explorer, the wizard will not start. To start the wizard, right-click the Internet Explorer icon, click Properties, and then in the Internet Properties dialog box, click the Connections tab. Click Setup to start the wizard. You can also click the Start button, point to Programs, point to Accessories, point to Communications, and then click Internet Connection Wizard.

2 Click the I Want To Transfer My Existing Internet Account To This Computer (My Telephone Line Is Connected To My Modem) option, and then click Next.

A list of phone numbers for the Microsoft Internet Referral Service is displayed.

3 Click any one of the phone numbers, and then click Next.

The wizard connects you to an online listing of national ISPs in your area. Local ISPs are not listed.

4 Click the My Internet Service Provider Is Not Listed option, and then click Next.

The Manual Internet Account Setup screen is displayed, explaining that you will need to manually enter your ISP information.

5 Click Next.

The Step 1 Of 3: Internet Account Connection Information screen is displayed.

tip

Some ISPs require that you change the advanced settings for your computer. Your ISP will alert you if this is necessary and supply the additional information. If you select the Yes option on the Step 1 Of 3 screen, the wizard will prompt you through entering advanced settings information such as connection type, and IP and DNS addresses.

6 In the boxes provided, type the area code and telephone number that your ISP provided you.

important

If you need to dial an area code but the number is not a long-distance number, enter the area code in the Telephone Number box with the telephone number, rather than in the Area Code box. For example, you can enter 555-111-1234 in the Telephone Number box. If you enter 555 in the Area Code box, Windows will assume that the number is long distance and will dial "1" before dialing the number.

If you need to change the country/region settings, select the correct location from the list.

7 Make sure that the information in the Country/Region Name And Code box is correct, and then click Next.

The Step 2 Of 3: Internet Account Logon Information screen is displayed.

8   In the User Name box and Password box, type the name and password information provided by your ISP, and then click Next.

The Step 3 Of 3: Configuring Your Computer screen is displayed.

tip

In the Step 3 Of 3: Configuring Your Computer screen, the Internet Connection Wizard typically uses your ISP's phone number as the name of your connection. It's usually a good idea to use a more informative name, especially if you have more than one Internet connection, so that you can easily identify the connection you want to use.

9   In the Connection Name box, accept the default name or type a new name for your connection, and then click Next.

The Set Up Your Internet Mail Account screen is displayed. You are asked if you want to set up an Internet mail account.

For information on setting up an e-mail account, see "Setting Up Outlook Express" later in this lesson.

10   Click No, and then click Next.

The Completing The Internet Connection Wizard screen is displayed. The To Connect To The Internet Immediately, Select This Box And Then Click Finish check box is selected.

11   Click Finish.

The Connect To dialog box appears. The connection information you entered in the wizard is displayed.

The steps for connecting to the Internet are discussed in "Using Dial-Up Networking to Set Up Additional Online Connections" later in this lesson.

12   If you want your password to be entered automatically, select the Save Password check box.

13   Type your password, and then click Connect to start Internet Explorer.

14   On the File menu, click Close.

The Auto Disconnect dialog box appears.

tip

You can also right-click the Dial-Up Networking icon on the System Tray, and then click Disconnect.

Dial-Up Networking

15   Click Disconnect Now.

tip
If you want to duplicate your Internet settings on another computer, you can use the Internet Connection Wizard to copy the settings of your already-set-up computer to a floppy disk that you can then use to set up the other computer.

Setting Up MSN and Other National Internet Service Providers

If you want to use a national Internet service provider like MSN or America Online (AOL), you can set up some of them directly from the Microsoft Windows Millennium Edition desktop. A Setup MSN Internet Access icon is included on the desktop; to set up MSN, just double-click the icon and work through the MSN Internet Access 5.0 Setup Wizard. You can also use the MSN Wizard if you want to set up an existing MSN account on your computer.

Windows provides shortcuts to other national services in the Online Services folder on the desktop. To set up one of these services, double-click the icon representing the service you want to try, and then work through the setup wizard.

Exploring New Features of Microsoft Internet Explorer 5.5

If you have been using Microsoft Internet Explorer 4.0 (IE 4.0) or earlier versions, you will find new features and enhanced usability of existing features in Microsoft Internet Explorer 5.5 (IE 5.5). For information on using Internet Explorer 5.5, see Internet Explorer 5.5 Help.

Feature	Version 5.5
Previewing printed versions of Web sites	You can preview how printed versions of Web pages will look before you print by using the Print Preview command on the File menu.

Feature	Version 5.5
Importing and exporting information	The Import/Export Wizard imports and exports Favorites links and cookies from Internet Explorer to or from other programs or files. The wizard is available on the File menu.
Using Internet Explorer tools	A Tools menu has been added, making it easier to find Internet Explorer tools and services such as Windows Update, e-mail, and links related to the currently open Web page.
Working with Favorites	The Organize Favorites dialog box has been redesigned to make it easier to organize and manage Favorites links.
Viewing pages offline	When you add a Web page to your Favorites list, you can mark it to be available offline.
Searching	Use the Search Assistant to specify the kind of search you want to do; for example, you can search for Web pages, e-mail addresses, businesses, and maps. You can also easily customize search settings, such as changing search providers. To open the Search Assistant, click Search on the toolbar.
Viewing list of visited sites	You can customize the History display to view the History list by date, site, most visited site, or by the order in which the sites were visited. To open History, click History on the toolbar.
Connecting to Multiple ISPs	If you have Internet accounts with more than one ISP, you can easily switch among the connections, change properties for each, and set the default connection on the Internet Options Connect tab. To open Internet Options, on the Tools menu, click Internet Options.
Accessing MSN Messenger Service	You can use the Messenger icon on the toolbar to instantly connect to the MSN Messenger Service.

Using Dial-Up Networking to Set Up Additional Online Connections

You can always start the Internet Connection Wizard again to set up additional Internet connections. However, a more direct method for setting up a connection is to go directly to Dial-Up Networking. In Dial-Up Networking, you can set up a connection as well as change connection properties for existing connections. Before you create a new connection, make sure that you have the phone number, user name, and password for the connection that you want to set up.

You have discovered a new local ISP that offers a free Internet connection. In this exercise, you decide to set up a new connection so that you can try out the new service. Then, you log on to the Internet using the new connection.

You can also click the Start button, point to Settings, and then click Dial-Up Networking.

1   Double-click the My Computer icon, and then click the Dial-Up Networking link.

The Dial-Up Networking folder opens, displaying your existing connection.

2   Double-click the Make New Connection icon to start the Make New Connection Wizard.

You can also click the Create button on the Standard Buttons toolbar.

3   In the Type A Name For The Computer You Are Dialing box, type a name for the new connection.

Make sure that you choose a connection name that will help you identify the connection.

4   Click Next, and then in the boxes provided, type the area code and phone number you want your modem to dial.

important

If you need to dial an area code but the number is not a long-distance number, enter the area code in the Telephone Number box with the telephone number, rather than in the Area Code box. For example, you can enter 555-111-1234 in the Telephone Number box. If you enter 555 in the Area Code box, Windows will assume that the number is long distance and will dial "1" before dialing the number.

5   Click Next, and then click Finish.

6   Double-click the icon of the new connection that you just created.

   The Connect To dialog box appears.

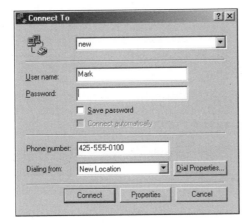

You can also click Dial on the Standard toolbar.

7   In the Password box, type your password, and then click Connect.

   Your browser starts and connects to the Internet. Your default home page is displayed.

8   Type the Internet address of the new ISP, and then press Enter.

   The home page for the ISP is displayed in your browser.

9   On the File menu, click Close, and then in the Auto Disconnect dialog box, click Disconnect Now.

   Your modem hangs up, and your computer is disconnected from the Internet.

tip

If you want Windows to remember your password so that you don't have to type it each time you connect to the Internet, select the Save Password check box. If you want Windows to connect to the ISP immediately after you double-click the Internet Connection icon, select the Connect Automatically check box.

Making Changes to Your Dial-Up Connection

You should not need to change the default dial-up settings; however, if you do need to make changes, you should check with your ISP or consult Windows Help before making the changes. Following is a list of routine changes that you can safely change on your own:

- Identifying your default connection. To make a connection your default Internet connection, in the Dial-Up Networking folder, right-click the dial-up connection icon that you want as your default connection, and then on the shortcut menu, click Set As Default. Your default connection is dialed when you start your browser or your e-mail program.

- Changing dial-up phone numbers. If you need to change the phone number for a connection, in the Dial-Up Networking folder, right-click the dial-up connection icon of the connection that you want to change, and then click Properties. Change the phone numbers on the General tab.

- Changing the disconnect settings. If your modem connection is slow, you might find that it disconnects unexpectedly if the idle setting is set too low. In the Dial-Up Networking folder, right-click the dial-up connection icon of the connection that you want to change, and then click Properties. Click the Dialing tab, and then make sure that the Enable Idle Disconnect check box is selected. In the Disconnect If Idle For box, increase the setting. The higher the setting, the longer your modem will remain connected when it is not sending or receiving data.

- Changing connection settings. If you are having trouble connecting to the Internet, try changing the Advanced Port settings so that your computer connects at a slower speed. In Control Panel, double-click the Modems icon, click Properties, click the Connection tab, and then click Port Settings. In the Receive Buffer box and Transmit Buffer box, change the setting to Medium or Low.

■ Dialing from an extension. If you need to dial an outside line before your modem can dial the ISP number, in the Dial-Up Networking folder, double-click the dial-up connection icon of the connection that you want to change, and in the Connect To dialog box, click Dial Properties. Enter your dialing information in the When Dialing From Here area of the Dialing Properties dialog box. You can also get to Dialing Properties by double-clicking the Telephony icon in Control Panel.

■ If your ISP connection number is in a different area code but not a long-distance number, you can set up the connection so that your modem does not dial "1" before dialing the ISP number. In the Dialing Properties dialog box, click Area Code Rules, and in the When Calling To Other Area Codes area, click New, and then type the area code your modem dials.

Setting Up and Removing Content Advisor Ratings

The Internet provides access to a wealth of information, but if your children are using the Internet, you might be concerned about the kind of information they are exposed to. The guiding principle for Web content is "anything goes," so exercising some control over the kind of Web content that children can view on your home computer can be a prudent decision.

Using the Microsoft Internet Explorer Content Advisor, you can control the kind of Web content users view on your computer. When you set up Content Advisor ratings, which are somewhat like movie ratings, Content Advisor screens out certain kinds of content, such as violence and offensive language. You can also assign a Supervisor password to the Content Advisor so that adults can bypass the ratings you have set up. If the Supervisor password option is selected and you encounter a Web site that does not meet the ratings standards or does not have a rating, a message appears indicating that you cannot view the page, but a password prompt also appears to allow you to circumvent the ratings system. If the Supervisor password option is not selected, the password prompt will not appear. The following table describes Content Advisor settings located in the Content Advisor dialog box. Refer to Internet Explorer Help for further information.

On this tab	You can
Ratings	Change rating levels for Web language, nudity, sex, and violence. See the following exercise for more detail.
Approved Sites	Specify Web sites that can and cannot be viewed.
General	Set password options and rating systems. See the following exercise for more detail.
Advanced	Set up advanced ratings systems.

In this exercise, you decide that you want to set up Content Advisor to prohibit viewing of certain kinds of content. You also want to set up a Content Advisor password so that you can turn Content Advisor ratings off when adults are using the Internet.

You do not have to be connected to the Internet to set up the Content Advisor.

1   On the Windows Me desktop, right-click the Internet Explorer icon, and then click Properties.

The Internet Properties dialog box appears.

2   Click the Content tab, and then in the Content Advisor area, click Enable.

The Content Advisor dialog box appears.

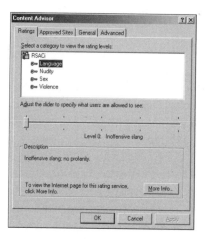

tip

The ratings are based on a Recreational Software Advisory Council (RSAC) system maintained by the Internet Content Rating Association (ICRA). To learn more about the ratings, click More Info in the Description area.

3   On the Ratings tab, make sure that the Language category is selected, and then move the Adjust The Slider To Specify What Users Are Allowed To See slider to Level 1: Mild Expletives.

Level 1 allows mild expletives or mild terms for bodily functions.

By default, the ratings are all set to Level 0.

4   Click Violence.

The default settings is Level 0, No Violence.

5   Move the Adjust The Slider To Specify What Users Are Allowed To See slider to Level 1: Fighting.

Level 1 allows Web content that depicts creatures injured or killed and damage to realistic objects.

6   Click the General tab, and then make sure that the Supervisor Can Type A Password To Allow Users To View Restricted Content check box is selected.

Users can type a password in the Supervisor Can Type A Password To Allow Users To View Restricted Content check box to circumvent the ratings.

tip

If you do not set up a password on the General tab, you will be prompted to set up a password when you exit the Content Advisor dialog box.

7   Click Change Password.

The Change Supervisor Password dialog box appears. Because you have not set up a password, you will not enter anything in the Old Password box.

8   Press Tab, and in the New Password box, type a password, press Tab, and then type the password again.

9   Click OK, and then click OK again.

The General tab is displayed.

10   Click OK, type your Supervisor password, and then click OK.

A message explaining that Content Advisor has been enabled is displayed.

11   Click OK twice.

tip

To disable the Content Advisor, on the Content tab of the Internet Options dialog box, click Disable. You will be prompted to enter your supervisor password before the content ratings are disabled. To change Content Advisor settings once Content Advisor has been enabled, in the Internet Options dialog box, click Settings in the Content Advisor area, and then type your supervisor password to access the Content Advisor dialog box.

Viewing Web Pages Offline

If you view a certain Web page frequently, but do not want to connect to the Internet every time to view it, you can set up the page as an offline Web page in Microsoft Internet Explorer to view later when you are not connected to the Internet. For example, if you often read an online advice column about gardening, you might not want to spend the time while you are online reading the page. Rather than having to connect to the Internet to view the Web page, you can set up the Web page as an offline Web page to view later, when you are not online. Whenever you are online, you can **synchronize** the page so that you can view the latest version after disconnecting from the Internet. By synchronizing offline Web pages, you can see what has changed on the Web page since you last viewed it.

In this exercise, you want to view your favorite Web page offline, so you decide to set up the page as an offline Web page that you synchronize when you connect to the Internet.

important

You must use Internet Explorer for this exercise. Other browsers might not support offline Web pages or might set them up differently.

1   On the Windows Me desktop, double-click the Internet Explorer icon, and then connect to your ISP.

Do not use your home page for this exercise.

2   In the Address bar, type the address of the Web page that you want to view offline, and then press Enter.

The Web page is displayed in your browser.

3   On the Favorites menu, click Add To Favorites.

The Add Favorite dialog box appears.

4   Select the Make Available Offline check box, and then click Customize. The Offline Favorite Wizard appears.

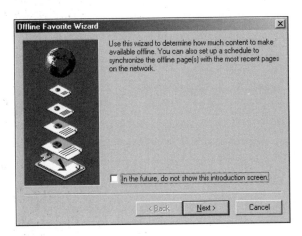

5   Click Next, make sure that No is selected, and then click Next.

tip

If you are connecting with a standard modem and telephone line, it is a good idea to download the page only. Downloading page links might take a considerable amount of time.

6   Make sure that the Only When I Choose Synchronize From The Tools Menu option is selected, and then click Next.

The page will not be updated automatically.

If you want to keep other users from viewing the offline Web page, select Yes, and then type a password.

7   Make sure that No is selected when prompted for a password, click Finish, and then click OK.

A message indicating that the Web page is synchronizing is displayed. The Synchronizing dialog box appears, and the Web site is synchronized.

Dial-Up Networking

8   On the File menu, click Close, right-click the Dial-Up Networking icon on the System Tray, and then click Disconnect.

9   Double-click the Internet Explorer icon, and then in the Connect To dialog box, click Work Offline.

In the Favorites folder, only offline Web pages are available when you are working offline or disconnected from the Internet.

10   On the Favorites menu, click the offline Web page that you set up.

The Web page is displayed.

11   On the File menu, click Close.

tip

To change the synchronization settings, right-click the page link on the Favorites menu, click Properties, and then in the Properties dialog box, click the Schedule tab. To set up the Web page to be synchronized automatically when you are connected to the Internet, click Using The Following Schedule(s), click Edit, and then click the Schedule tab.

Setting Up Outlook Express

For information on setting up multiple e-mail identities, see "Setting Up Outlook Express for Multiple Users" later in this lesson.

Microsoft Outlook Express 5.5 is the e-mail program that comes with Microsoft Windows Millennium Edition. Outlook Express can be set up for multiple users, which can be very useful if several family members are using it for e-mail. For example, you can set up an identity for each user so that each user has a personal set of e-mail folders, making it easy to keep messages intended for one person separate from those intended for another. You can also set up multiple e-mail accounts. If your spouse or partner has an account with another ISP, for example, both of you can set up your accounts in Outlook Express.

In this exercise, you want to set up Outlook Express so that you can send and receive e-mail messages.

important

Before you set up Outlook Express, make sure that you have your e-mail address and the address for your e-mail server. These are available from your ISP. If your ISP provides two e-mail server addresses, one for a **POP3** server and a second for an **SMTP** server, then you will need both numbers to set up Outlook Express.

1   On the desktop, double-click the Outlook Express icon.

The Internet Connection Wizard starts.

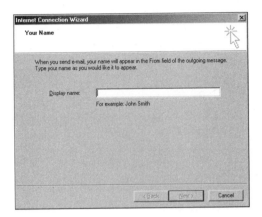

tip

The Internet Connection Wizard only starts the first time you start Outlook Express. If the wizard does not start, on the Outlook Express Tools menu, click Accounts, click Add, and then click Mail.

Consider your display name carefully. It is the name that will display in the From box in your outgoing e-mail messages.

2   In the Display Name box, type your display name, and then click Next.

    You are prompted to enter your e-mail address.

3   Make sure that the I Already Have An E-Mail Address That I'd Like To Use option is selected, in the E-Mail Address box, type your e-mail address, and then click Next.

    The E-Mail Server Names screen appears.

4   In the Incoming Mail (POP3, IMAP Or HTTP) Server box, type the POP3 server address that your ISP provided, and then press Tab.

    The pointer moves to the Outgoing Mail Server box. Your mail is held until you make a connection and request your e-mail messages.

important

The content of the E-Mail Server Names screen might vary, depending on how your ISP handles Internet connections. For example, if you are setting up an MSN Hotmail e-mail account, the necessary information is automatically entered in the screen, so you can click Next to proceed to the next wizard screen. If you are unsure what to enter in this screen, check with your ISP.

5   In the Outgoing Mail (SMTP) Server box, type the SMTP server address that your ISP provided, and then click Next.

The Internet Mail Logon screen appears. The account name is entered for you.

If your ISP requires you to use Secure Password Authentication, select the Log On Using Secure Password Authentication (SPA) check box.

6   In the Password box, type your ISP account password, and then click Next.

The final screen of the wizard appears, indicating that you have successfully entered the required information.

tip

If you want your password to be entered for you when you connect, select the Remember Password check box.

If you started the Internet Connection Wizard from within Outlook Express, you will need to close the Internet Accounts dialog box.

7   Click Finish to complete your account set up.

important

If a message asking if you want to go online is displayed, click Yes. If you are setting up a Hotmail account and a message asking if you want to download folders from your e-mail sever is displayed, click No.

8   Click Send/Recv.

The Dial-Up Connection dialog box appears.

To quit Outlook Express and log off the Internet, on the File menu, click Exit.

9   In the Password box, type your password, and then click Connect.

Outlook Express connects to the Internet and downloads any waiting e-mail messages from your ISP's e-mail server.

Setting Up Outlook Express for Multiple Users

For information on setting up your first ISP account using the Internet Connection Wizard, see "Setting Up Outlook Express" earlier in this lesson.

If you use more than one ISP or more than one e-mail account from an ISP, you can set up the additional e-mail account just as you have set up the first account. However, if more than one person uses the same e-mail account in your house, you can set up identities for each of them. When you log on using your personal identity in Microsoft Outlook Express, you see only the e-mail messages and contacts in the Address Book for your identity. This way, you avoid getting your e-mail messages and Address Book contacts confused with another user's, and you can organize your e-mail folders to suit your own needs.

You can also create an identity from the Address Book. See Lesson 4, "Using Windows for Work and Play."

In this exercise, you and your spouse will be using the same e-mail account on the same computer, so you decide that you will create an identity for your spouse so that it will be easier for each of you to manage your own e-mail messages and contacts.

important

When you set up more than one identity in Outlook Express, any incoming e-mail messages will be received in the active identity, unless each person is using a separate e-mail account. For example, if your identity is active and you download e-mail messages, you will receive both your spouse's mail and your mail in your Inbox. To move the mail from one account to another, you need to drag it to the desktop, switch identities, and then drag the mail into the Inbox of the other identity.

For a demonstration of how to set up Microsoft Outlook Express for multiple users, in the Multimedia folder on the Microsoft Windows Me Step by Step CD-ROM, double-click OEMultipleUsers.

1   On the File menu, point to Identities, and then click Add New Identity.

The New Identity dialog box appears.

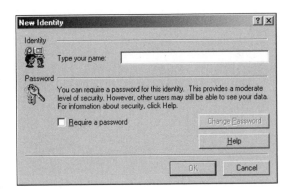

2   In the Type Your Name box, type **Charles** and then select the Require A Password check box.

The Enter Password dialog box appears.

3   Type **CA** and then press Tab.

4   Enter the password again, and then click OK twice.

A message asking if you want to switch to the new identity is displayed.

5   Click Yes.

The Internet Connection Wizard starts.

tip

If you set up a new identity that will use a separate e-mail account, you will need to set up a dial-up connection for that account. See "Using Dial-Up Networking to Set Up Additional Online Connections" earlier in this lesson.

6   In the Display Name box of the Your Name screen, type **Charles** and then click Next.

You are prompted to enter your e-mail address.

7   Make sure that the I Already Have An E-Mail Address That I'd Like To Use option is selected. In the E-Mail Address box, type your e-mail address, and then click Next.

The e-mail address entered here is for demonstration purposes only.

8   In the E-Mail Name box, type **charles@fun^s.net** click Next, and then click Yes when asked if you want to proceed with an invalid e-mail address.

9   Click Yes.

You are asked for your e-mail server names.

important

You cannot use nonalphabetic or nonnumeric characters, such as $ or %, in an e-mail address. The exercises in this book use invalid e-mail addresses to avoid inadvertently using an existing address. During this exercise, you will encounter messages informing you that the e-mail address and server names are invalid. When the messages appear, click Yes to continue with the exercise. You will be able to set up the account and continue with the exercise, but you will not be able to use the account to connect to the Internet.

tip

For more information on setting up an e-mail account, see "Setting Up Outlook Express" earlier in this lesson.

You can set up an account with MSN Hotmail, a free e-mail service. There is no charge for the account, but you need to use your existing ISP to connect to the service. To set up a Hotmail account, click the I'd Like To Sign Up For A New Account From option in the Internet E-Mail Address screen of the Internet Connection Wizard. Or, on the Outlook Express Tools menu, click New Account Signup.

10 In the Incoming Mail (POP3, IMAP Or HTTP) Server box, type
pop3.email.charles@fun^s.net and then press Tab.

The pointer moves to the Outgoing Mail (SMTP) Server box.

11 Type **smtp.email.charles@fun^s.net** and then click Next.

12 Click Yes twice when asked if you want to proceed with an invalid server
name.

The Internet Mail Logon screen appears. The account name has been entered.

13 In the Password box, type **CA** and then click Next.

The final screen of the wizard appears, indicating that you have successfully
entered the required information.

14 Click Finish.

Outlook Express switches to the new identity. The Outlook Express title bar
indicates which identity is active.

Managing Outlook Express Identities

If you have set up identities in Microsoft Outlook Express, you can easily
switch among them and make changes to the identity settings. You can do
the following with existing identities in Outlook Express:

- Log off an identity and switch to another.
- Change identity passwords.
- Delete an identity.
- Set the identity that will be active when you start Outlook Express.

Logging Off and Switching Identities

- To log off an identity and quit Outlook Express, on the File menu, click
Exit And Log Off Identity. Or, on the File menu, click Switch Identity, and
then click Log Off Identity.

- To switch to a different identity, on the File menu, click Switch Identity.
Select another identity in the list, type the password in the Password
box, click OK, and then click No.

(continued)

continued

Changing Identity Passwords

1   On the File menu, point to Identities, and then click Manage Identities.

2   Make sure that your identity is selected in the Identities list, and then click Properties.

3   Click Change Password.

4   Type your old password, press Tab, type your new password, press Tab, type your new password again, and then click OK twice.

Deleting an Identity

1   To save e-mail messages before deleting an identity, copy the messages to the desktop, log on to another identity, and then copy the messages for that identity first.

2   Make sure that you are logged on to an identity other than the one you want to delete. In the Identities list, select the identity you want to remove, and then click Remove.

Setting the Main Default Identity

1   On the File menu, point to Identities, and then click Manage Identities.

tip

The identity you select will only be active when you start Outlook Express if you have logged off when that identity was active or, if another identity was active, you chose Exit And Log Off Identity on the File menu.

2   Select the Use This Identity When Starting A Program check box, click the down arrow, and then select the identity that you want to be active when you start Outlook Express.

3   Click Close.

Accessing and Using Newsgroups with Outlook Express

A newsgroup is a collection of e-mail messages about a certain topic that have been sent, or posted, by individual users to a news server. The newsgroup consists of messages plus follow-up messages. For instance, in a newsgroup devoted to home repair topics, a user might post a message asking for advice on repairing a hot water heater. Other users would then post replies, offering comments or possible solutions.

Anyone can post messages to a newsgroup, and you can find newsgroups on just about any subject. Some newsgroups are moderated, which means that someone reviews the questions and deletes messages that are inappropriate; other newsgroups are not moderated.

Microsoft Outlook Express contains a newsreader, which is a program that you can use to access newsgroups. First you need to make sure that your ISP offers links to news servers. Then, you can download a list of newsgroups, search for one that looks interesting, and read and post messages to it. If you really like the newsgroup, you can become a newsgroup member by subscribing to it, which means that it will be displayed in your Outlook Express Folders list, making it easy to access.

To complete this exercise, you need to call your ISP to get the name of the news server you can connect to. You can also search for "newsgroups" on the Internet to find the address of a newsgroup to use for this exercise.

In this exercise, you want to find a newsgroup that will offer discussion on one of your interests. Then, you set up a newsgroup account, search for a newsgroup, and then subscribe to it.

tip

Newsgroups are available only to the identity in which they are set up. If you want to view a newsgroup in another identity, you need to switch to that identity, and then set up the newsgroup again.

1   Make sure that Outlook Express is running, and then in the Folders list, click Outlook Express.

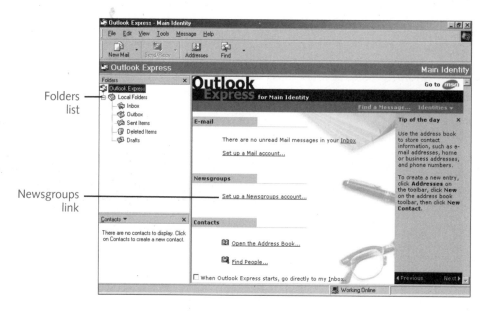

Folders list

Newsgroups link

The Information Viewer is the large pane on the right side of the Outlook Express window.

2   In the Information Viewer, click the Set Up A Newsgroups Account link.

The Internet Connection Wizard starts.

3   Make sure that your display name is entered in the Display Name box, and then click Next.

The Internet News E-Mail Address screen appears.

4   Make sure that your e-mail address is displayed in the E-Mail Address box, and then click Next.

The Internet News Server Name dialog box appears.

5   In the News (NNTP) Server box, type the address of your news server, and then click Next.

A message informing you that you have successfully entered the required information is displayed.

important

If your ISP requires you to log on to your news server, select the My News Server Requires Me To Log On check box. Then, click Next, and type your account name and password. If required by your ISP, select the Log On Using Secure Network Authentication check box. Finally, click Next, and then continue with step 6.

6 Click Finish.

A message asking if you want to download newsgroups from the account that you just added is displayed.

You only need to download the newsgroup list once.

7 Click Yes.

The Connect To dialog box appears.

8 If necessary, type your user name and password, and then click Connect.

Your computer connects to the Internet. A message informing you that newsgroups are downloading is displayed. After a few minutes, a list of newsgroups is displayed in the Newsgroup Subscriptions dialog box.

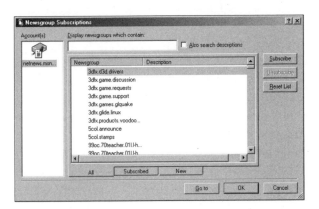

9 In the Display Newsgroups Which Contain box, type a keyword for a topic that interests you.

A list of related newsgroups is displayed.

10 Select a newsgroup, and then click Go To.

A list of messages in the newsgroup is displayed.

11 Click a message to read it. To expand a list of messages, click the plus sign (+) next to a message.

To post a new message, click New Post on the toolbar. To reply to a message, click Reply or Reply Group.

12 To subscribe to the newsgroup, in the Folders list, right-click the newsgroup name, and then click Subscribe.

The Newsgroup icon is highlighted to indicate that you have subscribed to it.

13 On the File menu, click Exit, and then click Disconnect Now.

Outlook Express quits, and your modem disconnects from the Internet.

---

tip

The Outlook Express newsreader provides a number of options that make viewing newsgroup messages efficient. For example, you can view newsgroup messages offline, and you can hide messages that you have already read. For more information on using the Outlook Express newsreader, see Outlook Express Help.

Using MSN Instant Messenger Service

MSN Instant Messenger Service is an e-mail program that sends e-mail messages in real-time—that is, as soon as someone sends you an **instant message**, it appears immediately in your e-mail program. You do not have to download the message as you would an ordinary e-mail message. MSN Messenger Service is similar to **chat**, except that with chat, anyone with an Internet connection can view messages from the chat participants and send messages to them. MSN Messenger Service is private; you determine who participates, and the only people who know about the Instant Messenger conversation are those you notify.

For more information on setting up an MSN Hotmail account, see "Setting Up Outlook Express for Multiple Users" earlier in this lesson.

To use the MSN Messenger Service, you first must have an MSN Hotmail account, which is free. If you do not have a Hotmail account, you can sign up for one as you install the MSN Messenger Service. Next, you set up MSN Messenger Service on your computer using the MSN Messenger Service Wizard. Then you can log on to the messaging services and send and receive instant messages. Instant messages are limited to 400 characters.

For more information on MSN Messenger Service, see MSN Messenger Service Help after you have set up the service. Or go to *http://messenger.msn.com/*.

Setting Up MSN Messenger Service and Logging On

1   Click the Start button, point to Programs, point to Accessories, point to Communications, and then click MSN Messenger Service.

2   If you do not have a Hotmail account, click Get A Passport, and then connect to the Internet. Sign up for an account, and then return to the MSN Messenger Service Wizard. If you already have a Hotmail account, click Next.

3   Type your Hotmail e-mail address and password, click Next, and then click Finish. You will be prompted to connect to the Internet.

4   Click Connect. Once you are connected to the Internet, you are prompted to log on to the MSN Messenger Service. Type your password, and then click OK to log on.

5   To add the e-mail address of a contact to your Contacts list, click Add, click By E-Mail Address, click Next, type the person's Hotmail e-mail address, click Next, click No if you don't want to send MSN Messenger instructions to your recipient, and then click Finish.

Sending an Instant Message

1   To send an instant message, the person or persons you want to send the message to must be logged on to MSN Messenger Service. In MSN Messenger Service, double-click the name or names.

2   Type your message in the lower part of the window, and then click Send.

3   To send a message to someone not in your list, click Send, click Other, and then type the person's Hotmail e-mail address.

Lesson Wrap-Up

In Lesson 2, you learned how to set up an Internet connection using the Internet Connection Wizard and Dial-Up Networking. You defined Content Advisor settings for Microsoft Internet Explorer and learned to view Web pages offline. Next, you set up Microsoft Outlook Express 5.5 and Outlook Express identities for family members. Finally, you learned how to access Internet newsgroups.

If you are continuing to the next lesson:

1   Close any open windows before continuing.

2   If you want to delete the Hotmail account you set up in this lesson, start Outlook Express if you are not logged on. On the Tools menu, click Accounts, select the account, and then click Remove.

3   To unsubscribe to the newsgroup you subscribed to in this lesson, open the Newsgroup Subscriptions dialog box, select the newsgroup, and then click Unsubscribe.

If you are not continuing to other lessons:

1   Follow the steps in the previous section to delete your Hotmail account and newsgroup subscription.

2   If you are finished using your computer for now, log off Windows.

3   If you will not be using your computer for a long time, shut down Windows.

Glossary

chat   A real-time exchange of dialog using a computer, which is much like holding a conversation online. When users chat, they typically send brief messages of a few sentences or less that are immediately displayed on the recipient's computer. Some chats focus on particular subjects; others do not. Any user with the proper Internet connection can participate in a chat. Often they are not monitored or refereed, so in some cases, chat content might not be suitable for children. ISPs, particularly national ISPs, typically support chat and provide the necessary connections to take part in them.

instant message   A form of e-mail similar to chat that is usually restricted to a self-defined group of participants. For example, users can set up an instant message group that consists of coworkers, neighbors, or family members. As in chat, instant messages occur in real-time, and the messages are restricted to a few sentences. Usually, national ISPs, like MSN or AOL, provide instant message services.

Internet service provider (ISP)   A business that sells Internet connectivity services. ISPs function as the gateway between users and the Internet. When you sign up with an ISP, you typically receive an e-mail address and a telephone number that your modem dials to connect to the Internet. Some ISPs, like MSN and AOL, are national services. Depending on where you live, you might have local ISPs that provide Internet connections. Some locations might also have ISPs that offer free Internet connections and e-mail, but their services are often limited.

newsgroup   An Internet forum that consists of e-mail messages (called *posts*) and follow-up replies to the messages. Newsgroups are typically focused on a particular subject, like computers or parenting. Each newsgroup is defined by a name that usually describes its subject in a series of increasingly narrow categories. An ISP typically provides access to newsgroups.

POP3 POP3 stands for Post Office Protocol. It is an alternative e-mail protocol used to serve intermittent dial-up connections to the Internet.

SMTP SMTP stands for Simple Mail Transfer Protocol. SMTP allows messages to be sent from one computer to another, even if the second computer has a different type of operating system.

synchronize To compare two versions of something, such as Web pages or documents, to make sure that they contain the same data. Once the comparison is made and differences are identified, one of the versions, usually the earliest version, is updated to match the other.

Quick Reference

To use the Internet Connection Wizard

1   After signing up with an ISP, right-click the Internet Explorer icon on the desktop, and then click Properties.

2   Click the Connections tab, and then click Setup.

3   Work through the steps in the wizard.

To use Dial-Up Networking to set up additional online connections

1   Double-click the My Computer icon, click the Dial-Up Networking link, and then double-click the Make New Connection icon.

2   Follow the steps in the Make New Connection Wizard.

To set up Content Advisor ratings

1   On the desktop, right-click the Internet Explorer icon, and then click Properties.

2   Click the Content tab, and then click Enable.

3   On the Ratings tab, select a rating category, and then move the slider to adjust the rating.

4   To set user options, click the General tab.

To view Web pages offline

1   On the desktop, double-click the Internet Explorer icon, and then connect to your ISP.

2   In the Address bar, type the address of the Web page that you want to view offline, and then press Enter.

3   On the Favorites menu, click Add To Favorites, select the Make Available Offline check box, and then click Customize.

4   Click Next, make sure that No is selected, and then click Next.

5   Make sure that the Only When I Choose Synchronize From The Tools Menu option is selected, click Next, make sure that No is selected, click Finish, and then click OK.

6   On the File menu, click Close, right-click the Internet Connection icon on the taskbar, and then click Disconnect.

7   Double-click the Internet Explorer icon, and in the Connect To dialog box, click Work Offline. On the Favorites menu, click the Offline Web page that you set up.

To set up Outlook Express

1   On the Quick Launch bar, click the Outlook Express icon.

2   Follow the steps in the Internet Connection Wizard.

To set up Outlook Express for multiple users

1   On the desktop, double-click the Outlook Express icon. On the File menu, point to Identities, and then click Add New Identity.

2   Type a name, select the Require A Password check box, and then type a password.

3   Type the password again, and then click OK twice.

4   Click Yes, and then follow the steps in the Internet Connection Wizard. Click the I Already Have An E-Mail Address That I'd Like To Use option to use your existing e-mail account.

To access and use newsgroups with Outlook Express

1   On the desktop, double-click the Outlook Express icon. In the Folders list, click Outlook Express.

2   In the Information Viewer, click the Set Up A Newsgroup Account link, and then follow the steps in the Internet Connection Wizard.

3   When a message asking if you want to download newsgroups is displayed, click Yes. Then, connect to the Internet.

4   In the Display Newsgroups Which Contain window, type the name of a topic in which you are interested.

5   After locating a newsgroup you want to subscribe to, in the Folders list, right-click the newsgroup, and then click Subscribe.

3

Using a Home Network

After completing this lesson, you will be able to:

**ESTIMATED
TIME
30 min.**

✔   *Share folders using a direct cable connection or a home network.*

✔   *Connect two computers with a serial or parallel cable.*

✔   *Transfer files between computers.*

✔   *Set up a computer network and share an Internet connection in your home.*

✔   *Use a home network to view and copy files.*

✔   *Use a shared Internet connection to connect a computer on a network to the Internet.*

Once you set up an Internet connection on your computer, your computer becomes an even more useful and entertaining tool. If you have more than one computer in your home, you can make all of your computers more useful by connecting them.

In this lesson, you will learn how to share folders so that you can view and use them on a **network**. Then, you will learn how to set up and use a direct connection to transfer files between two computers. Then, you will set up a home network and set up Internet Connection Sharing on the network. Finally, you'll learn how you can use a home network for transferring files and connecting to the Internet.

For additional information on installing practice files, see the "Using the Microsoft Windows Me Step by Step CD-ROM" section at the beginning of this book.

To complete the exercises in this lesson, you will need to use the Windows Me SBS folder and the files in the Family Photos folder. Before you can work with any of these exercise files, you must copy them from the Microsoft Windows Me Step by Step CD-ROM to your hard disk. If you plan on setting up a direct cable connection or home network, you will also need the following hardware: two computers, a **serial** or **parallel** cable for a direct cable connection, a home network kit installed, a blank floppy disk for setting up a home network, and a modem and an Internet connection for Internet connection sharing over a home network.

Sharing Folders

When you share a folder, you set up **permissions** so that other users on a network can view, read, and edit files in folders on your computer. You can set up folder sharing as you set up a direct cable connection or home network. However, it's easier if you set up folder sharing before setting up your connection because you don't have to restart your computer while you are setting up your connection.

You can share one or more folders or the entire content of your hard disk. Before you share any of your hard disk content, you should consider what you are giving others access to. It is easy to inadvertently give permission to read or even edit private documents. To share a folder or your hard disk icon in My Computer, you right-click the item you want to share, and then click Sharing. When you share a folder, you need to select the Access Type—for example, whether users can only view the contents of the shared folder or whether they can also edit it. You can also name the shared folder, add a comment, and assign a password to control access to shared folders. The table on the following page describes settings for shared folders.

important

If your computer is connected to the Internet, it is possible that others might be able to gain access to shared resources. You can help secure shared folders by setting up passwords for them. You might also consider other means of securing your computer, particularly if you are connected to the Internet for long periods of time. For more information, search for the terms "Network Security" in Windows Help. You can also search for the term "Internet Security" in Windows Help, and then click the MSN Safe Computing Forum link.

Share Option	Description
Share Name	You can type a new folder name. The new name will be used by other users who look for the folder over a network.
Comment	You can enter a comment to describe the folder contents. Other users can see the comment when they access the folder on a network.
Access Type:	
Read-Only	Other users can open and copy files and folders, but not modify or delete them.
Full	Other users can change, add, or remove files and folders.
Depends On Password	You can assign read-only privileges to some users and full access privileges to others. Each type of access requires a password.
Passwords:	
Read-Only Password	Controls read-only access.
Full Access Password	Controls full access.

For a demonstration of setting up folder sharing, in the Multimedia folder on the Microsoft Windows Me CD-ROM, double-click FolderSharing.

In this exercise, you decide to set up folder sharing before you set up a direct cable connection and a home network.

1   Click the Start button, point to Settings, and then click Control Panel to display the contents of the Control Panel folder.

2   Double-click the Network icon, and then click File And Print Sharing.

    The File And Print Sharing dialog box appears.

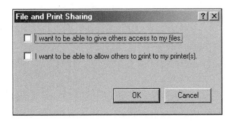

For more information about printer sharing, see "Setting Up a Home Network and Internet Connection Sharing on Another Computer" later in this lesson.

3   Select the I Want To Be Able To Give Others Access To My Files check box, and then click OK twice.

    A message indicating that you must restart your computer is displayed.

4   Click Yes to restart your computer.

5   At the Windows logon prompt, type your name and password, and then click OK.

The Windows Me desktop opens, displaying the contents of the Control Panel folder.

6   Close Control Panel. Double-click the My Computer icon, double-click the Local Disk icon, and then double-click the Windows Me SBS folder to display its contents.

tip

If you want others to have access to all the files and folders on the computer, you can share your entire hard disk.

7   Right-click the Family Photos folder, and then click Sharing.

The Family Photos Properties dialog box appears. The Sharing tab is displayed.

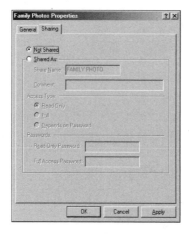

Shared folder

8   Click Shared As. In the Access Type area, click Full, and then click OK.

The standard folder icon for the Family Photos folder is replaced with the shared folder icon to indicate that the folder is shared.

tip
You can make shared folders password-protected by typing a password in the Full Access Password box. Users will need to type the password to view the contents of the folder. If you click the Depends On Password option in the Access Type area, you can assign a separate password for read-only and full access privileges.

9 Close the Windows Me SBS folder.

Setting Up a Direct Cable Connection Between Two Computers

For more information on compressing files, see Lesson 1, "Customizing Windows for Personal Use." For more information on compressing floppy disks, see Lesson 4, "Using Windows for Work and Play."

If you have two computers, you know that transferring files between them can be a lot of trouble. If you use the traditional floppy-disk method, you must copy the files to be transferred from one computer onto a floppy disk, physically transport the floppy disk to another computer, and then copy the files from the floppy disk to the second computer. If you own a desktop and a laptop computer, you probably have to transfer files quite often. And if the files are large, you might need more than one floppy disk, or you might need to compress the files or floppy disk before transferring the files.

Although using floppy disks to copy files is reliable, Microsoft Windows Millennium Edition provides a simpler method: connecting a cable from one computer to the other and then using the Direct Cable Connection Wizard to set up the connection. Of course, your computers need to be located close to each other; if they are located in different rooms of your house and you want to connect them, you should set up a home network.

For more information on home networks, see "Setting Up a Home Network and Sharing an Internet Connection" later in this lesson.

With a direct cable connection, you can copy files and gain access to any network that the other computer is connected to. For instance, you might view a letter located on the hard disk of the computer you are connected to, and then copy it to your computer. Or, if the main computer is located on a network, you can view folders on the network if you have sharing privileges.

important

It is important that you use the correct cable type. Standard parallel or serial cables will not work. You will need either a high-speed direct parallel cable or a PC-to-PC File Transfer serial cable. For information on purchasing a parallel cable, search for the term "Direct Cable Connection" in Windows Help. If you are purchasing a serial cable, contact your computer manufacturer or a computer parts vendor.

Before you set up a direct cable connection, you need to make sure that your computers have either a serial or parallel port, or connector, that you can use. Most printers are connected to parallel ports; monitors and some peripheral devices like game controllers sometimes use serial ports. You will also need a cable that has either a parallel connector on each end or a serial connector on each end. When you purchase a cable, make sure that you get the correct connector type—male or female—to plug into your computer. For example, if both ports on your computers are male connectors, make sure that the cable has female connectors on each end.

tip

If you do not have a spare serial or parallel port on your computer, you can temporarily unplug your printer or a serial device, or you can purchase a parallel or serial port adapter, which is similar to a circuit board that plugs into your computer.

important

Direct cable connection will not work if you connect a serial port to a parallel port.

When you set up your direct cable connection, one of your computers will be the **host** computer and the other the **guest** computer. The host is the computer that has the resources you want to use. For example, if you want to be able to connect to a network through your direct cable connection, the computer that has the network connection should be identified as the host. If you are connecting a desktop computer and a laptop, the desktop computer is usually the host.

In this exercise, your mother has just arrived for a visit and brought her laptop. You want to give her copies of the family photos you have stored on your hard disk. There are several files, so you decide to set up a direct cable connection using your desktop computer as the host.

important

To use Direct Cable Connection, the guest computer must be running Windows Me, Windows 98, Windows 95, or Windows for Workgroups.

If Direct Cable Connection doesn't appear on the Communications menu for either computer, you will need to install it. See Appendix B, "Installing Microsoft Windows Me."

1 Click the Start button, point to Programs, point to Accessories, point to Communications, and then click Direct Cable Connection.

The Direct Cable Connection Wizard appears.

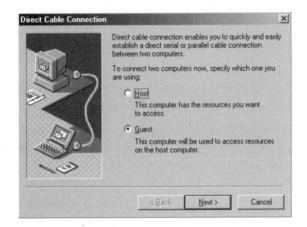

If you have just installed a serial or parallel adapter in your computer and it is not listed in the wizard, click Install New Ports.

2 Click Host, and then click Next.

Windows detects the ports installed on your computer and lists them in the wizard.

3 Click the port you want to use, connect the cable to both computers, and then click Next.

A message explaining that you have successfully set up the host computer and that you should set up the guest computer if you have not already done so is displayed.

tip
You can also create a password so that the guest computer must log on before accessing files on the host.

4 Click Finish, and then click Close.

Because the guest computer is not set up yet, you close Direct Cable Connection.

It's a good idea to quit all programs before running the wizard.

5 On the guest computer, click the Start button, point to Programs, point to Accessories, point to Communications, and then click Direct Cable Connection.

The Direct Cable Connection Wizard starts.

6 Click Guest, and then click Next.

Windows detects the ports installed on your computer and lists them in the wizard.

You must use the same port type on the guest computer as you used on the host computer.

7 Click the port you want to use.

8 Click Next.

A message explaining that you have successfully set up the guest computer is displayed.

9 Click Finish, and then click Close.

The guest computer is set up. A message indicating that the guest computer is trying to connect to the host is displayed.

10 Click Close.

You will not be able to connect yet. You will connect the computers and transfer files in the next exercise.

tip
If you want to change which computer is the host and which is the guest, select Start/Programs/Accessories/Communications, and then click Direct Cable Connection. Click Change to start the Direct Cable Connection Wizard again. You will also need to re-run the wizard on the other computer.

Using a Direct Cable Connection to Transfer Files

Now that you have the direct cable connection set up on both computers, you are ready to transfer files between them. To use the direct cable connection, you need to start the connection on each computer. Then, you must log the guest computer on to the host computer. Once the connection is established, a window appears on the guest computer that contains the shared folders on the host computer. You can drag items from the shared folder on the host computer to the guest computer, or you can drag items from the guest computer to the shared folder on the host computer.

In this exercise, you have the direct cable connection set up on your computer and your mother's computer, and you are ready to transfer the family photos.

important

Before you establish the connection between the two computers, you will need to find out the name of the host computer. On the host computer, open Control Panel, double-click the Network icon, and then click the Identification tab. The computer name will be listed in the Computer Name box.

1   On the host computer, click the Start button, point to Programs, point to Accessories, point to Communications, and then click Direct Cable Connection.

The Direct Cable Connection dialog box appears informing you that the host is ready to connect to the guest computer on the cable you have installed.

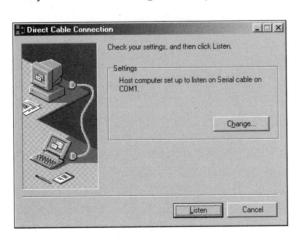

2   Click Listen.

A message indicating that the host is waiting to connect to the guest computer is displayed.

tip

If it takes you more than a few seconds to start Direct Cable Connection on the guest computer, you might see a message on the host computer indicating that it cannot connect to the guest. If that message appears, go ahead and start the connection on the guest, and then click OK in the message box on the host. The connection will be established between both computers.

3   On the guest computer, click the Start button, point to Programs, point to Accessories, point to Communications, and then click Direct Cable Connection.

The Direct Cable Connection dialog box appears informing you that the guest computer is ready to connect to the host computer on the cable you have installed.

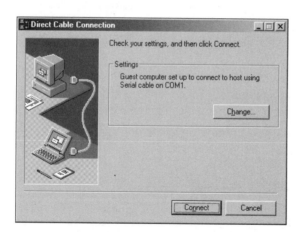

4   On the guest computer, click Connect.

A message indicating that the guest computer is connecting is displayed, and in a few seconds, the Direct Cable Connection dialog box on the host computer changes to indicate that it is connected to the guest computer.

For more information on sharing folders, see "Sharing Folders" earlier in this lesson.

5   On the guest computer, type the name of your host computer, and then click OK.

The host folder that contains the Family Photos folder is displayed, which is the folder you have shared on the host computer.

The folder name contains only 12 characters. File names displayed in the host folder are truncated to 12 characters.

6 On the guest computer, double-click the Family Photo folder, and then drag the Amy file to the desktop.

A copy of the file is placed on the desktop. You might have to drag the window out of the way to see it.

7 Close the shared folder.

8 On the guest computer, in the Direct Cable Connection dialog box, click Close, and then close the host folder that is open on your desktop.

The Direct Cable Connection is closed.

You might have to move the shared folder out of the way to see the Direct Cable Connection dialog box.

9 On the host computer, in the Direct Cable Connection dialog box, click Close.

Setting Up a Home Network and Sharing an Internet Connection

A direct cable connection is a simple solution to the problem of transferring files between two computers. However, the following are some drawbacks to direct cable connections:

- The connection can be slow, especially if you are using a serial cable and transferring large files.

- You can connect two computers only. You cannot use a direct connection to transfer files among several computers.

- A direct connection is only feasible if the two computers you want to connect are within a few feet of each other.

- A direct connection is intended primarily for transferring files. You do not have access to all resources on the host computer, such as an Internet connection.

If a direct cable connection doesn't suit your needs, you might want to set up a home network. You do need to purchase home network hardware to set up a home network, but you'll gain several distinct advantages:

- Home networks are usually much faster than direct cable connections, and you can connect more than two computers to the network, depending on the type of hardware you purchase.

- You can access and transfer files, but you can also share printers and other hardware, and Internet connections.

- If you have two computers that are located in different rooms, and you want to frequently share files and hardware, a home network can be an efficient choice.

To set up a home network, you need to purchase a **network adapter** for each computer in your network. The network adapter is either installed in your computer or is connected to it. Depending on the type of home network you set up, you might also need cabling to connect the computers, and a **hub**, or connector box, if you want to connect more than two computers. You can purchase home networking kits that provide all of the hardware you will need, as well as instructions for installing the hardware in your computer. The following illustration depicts a network that consists of four computers and a hub. Of course, you will need at least two computers—a **server** computer that is running Microsoft Windows Millennium Edition on which you set up home networking, and one or more additional computers.

tip

The terms *server* and *host* both refer to the primary computer on a network. The server or host provides access to other computers on the network and might provide services such as e-mail to the other computers. By convention, however, in Windows Me, the term *host* is used when referring to direct cable connections and Internet connection sharing; whereas, the term *server* is used when referring to home networking.

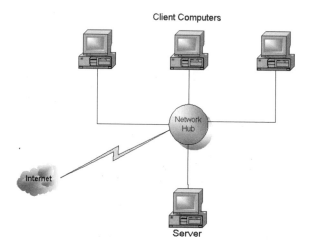

You can also find more information on home networks at www.microsoft.com/homenet.

Which kind of network you choose will depend on your preferences and your current system configuration. It's a good idea to research your options thoroughly by talking with knowledgeable vendors or your computer manufacturer before you choose a network for your home. Home networking technology is changing quickly, and more capable and efficient home networking hardware is entering the marketplace frequently. In general, there are several kinds of home networks available today.

Network Type	Description
Cable	Uses a special type of cable, called an *Ethernet cable*, to connect the networked computers.
Phone Line	Uses existing phone lines in your home instead of a separate cable to connect the networked computers.
Power Line	Uses the existing power lines in your home rather than cable or phone lines.
Wireless	Uses radio signals to connect the computers. Similar to a cordless telephone.

As you set up home networking, you can also set up Internet Connection Sharing (ICS). With ICS, computers on a network share a single Internet connection. For example, you can set up an Internet connection on your server computer and then set up the other computers to use the same connection to browse the Internet or send and receive e-mail messages. All the computers on the network can use the same Internet connection simultaneously.

The network server doesn't have to be the ICS host. Any computer on the network can be the ICS host.

important

If you are using a high-speed Internet connection with a hub such as a cable modem or Digital Subscriber Line (DSL), you will need two network adapters in your ICS host computer—the computer on which you first set up home networking. You connect one network adapter directly to the Internet connection and connect the other adapter to the hub. Your linked computers will be more secure; if other Internet users try to gain unauthorized access to your network, they will only be able to access your ICS host computer. For more information, search for the term "Home Network" in Windows Help, and then click the Home Networking With A Network Hub topic.

If the Home Networking Wizard is not displayed on the Communications menu, you will need to install it.

In this exercise, you want to permanently connect the two computers in your home, so you purchased a home networking kit and installed it following the manufacturer's directions. In addition, your family wants to use the Internet and send and receive e-mail messages from both computers. You do not want to go to the expense of setting up another connection, so you decide to share your Internet connection as you set up the home network.

If ICS is not installed on your computer, you will need to install it. For help installing Windows components, see Appendix B, "Installing Microsoft Windows Me."

tip

To verify that ICS is set up on your server computer, open Control Panel, and then double-click Add/Remove programs. Click the Windows Setup tab, and then double-click Communications. If the Internet Connection Sharing check box is not selected, you will have to install ICS before you run the Home Networking Wizard.

If you have already installed ICS, the Home Networking Wizard will start.

1   On your Windows Me computer that will be the **network server**, click the Start button, point to Programs, point to Accessories, point to Communications, and then click Home Networking Wizard.

The Home Networking Wizard starts.

2   Click Next to view the Internet Connection screen.

3   Make sure that the A Direct Connection To My ISP Using The Following Device option is selected and that the correct dial-up networking connection is displayed, and then click Next.

The Internet Connection Sharing screen appears.

4   Make sure that Yes is selected to let other computers share the Internet connection. Then, make sure that your home networking device is listed in the Select The Device That Connects This Computer To Your Home Network box, and then click Next.

The Establishing Internet Connection screen appears.

You do not need to change the default workgroup name.

5   In the Computer Name box, type a name to identify your computer on the network, and then click Next.

The Share Files And Printers screen appears.

6   Select the My Documents Folder And All Folders In It check box. Click Password adjacent to the selection you just made, type a password for the Shared Documents folder, press Tab, and type the password again. Click OK, and then click Next.

The Home Networking Setup Disk screen appears. You must create a setup disk to set up the other computers on your network.

You can share additional files or change sharing options after setting up your home network. See "Sharing Folders" earlier in this lesson.

7   Make sure that the Yes, Create A Home Networking Setup Disk option is selected, click Next, insert a blank floppy disk in your floppy drive, and then click Next again.

A message indicating that the setup disk is being created is displayed. When the copying is finished, the Completing The Home Networking Wizard appears.

8   Click Finish.

A message explaining that you must remove the floppy disk from the floppy drive and then restart your computer is displayed.

9   Remove the floppy disk, and then click Yes.

Your computer restarts.

10   At the Windows logon prompt, type your user name and password, and then click OK.

A message explaining that home networking is set up on your computer and that you must set up home networking on your other network computers is displayed.

tip
Run the Home Networking Wizard again if you need to change your home network settings or create another home networking setup disk.

Setting Up a Home Network and Internet Connection Sharing on Another Computer

Once you have home networking and ICS set up on the server computer, you must set them up on the other computers that you want to be part of your home network. Because you have created a setup disk, you simply insert that disk in each computer's floppy drive and run the setup program. When you are finished, home networking will be set up on each computer. You can view, move, and copy files among the computers and connect to the Internet on all networked computers, as well as other tasks.

In this exercise, you want to finish setting up your home network by installing home networking software on your second computer.

If you haven't created a home networking floppy disk, refer to the previous section, "Setting Up a Home Network and Sharing an Internet Connection."

1   Insert the home networking setup disk that you created from the server computer in your other computer's floppy drive.

2   Click the Start button, and then click Run.

    The Run dialog box appears.

3   In the Open box, Type **A:setup** and then click OK.

    The Home Networking Wizard starts.

4   Click Next.

    The Internet Connection screen appears. If the wizard is not installed, a message will appear that the Home Networking Wizard is being installed.

5   Make sure that the A Connection To Another Computer On My Home Network That Provides Direct Access To My Internet Service Provider (ISP) option is selected, and then click Next.

    The Computer And Workgroup Names screen appears.

6   In the Computer Name box, verify the current name or type a new computer name for this computer, and then click Next.

    The Share Files And Printers screen appears.

important

The computer name must be different from the name you used for your first computer. However, the workgroup name is the same name as the workgroup name you used for your first computer. Do not change the workgroup name; it must be identical to the name you used for the first computer.

The password can be different from the password you selected for the server computer.

7 Select the My Documents Folder And All Folders In It check box, click Password adjacent to the selection you just made, type a password for the Shared Documents folder, press Tab, type the password again, click OK, and then click Next.

For more information about printer sharing, see Lesson 7, "Backing Up Files and Adding Hardware."

tip
On the Share Files And Printers screen, If you have a printer connected to your **client** computer, it will be selected by default to share with other connected computers. If you do not want to share the printer with other connected computers, clear the check box next to the printer you don't want to share.

If requested to insert the Windows 98 CD, insert the CD, and then work through the prompts.

8 Click Finish to complete the home networking setup, remove the floppy disk from the floppy drive, and then click Yes to restart the computer.

9 After the computer restarts, at the Windows logon prompt, type your user name and password, and then click OK.

A message indicating that Home Networking is installed on the second computer is displayed.

Viewing and Copying Files over a Home Network

For help sharing files or folders, see "Sharing Folders" earlier in this lesson.

important
Before completing this exercise, you will need to share files or folders on your second computer. You can share any existing file or folder, such as My Documents, or even share the entire contents of your hard disk.

Once you have your home network set up, you can do a number of tasks, depending on your network type and your computer setup. A common task is to access files on other computers on the network. For example, you might find that the clip art you want to use in your report is on the computer that your kids are using. Rather than copying the clip art to a floppy disk and then copying it to your computer, you can simply copy the file over the network.

In this exercise, you have finished setting up your home network on both computers, and now you want to copy files from the older computer to your computer with Microsoft Windows Millennium Edition installed.

important

For more information on user profiles, see Lesson 1, "Customizing Windows for Personal Use."

For any linked computer to use resources on the network, the computer you're using and the computer whose resources you want to access must be logged on to Windows. At the Windows logon prompt, make sure that you type your user name, password, and workgroup name, and then click OK. If you do not have a profile set up on your computer, just click OK.

1   Make sure that you are logged on to Windows, and then on the client computer, double-click the Network Neighborhood icon.

The shared computers on the network are displayed in Network Neighborhood.

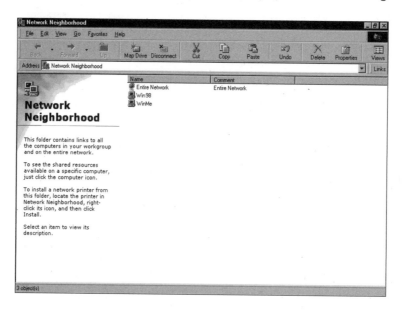

2   Double-click the shared computer whose files you want to view.

The computer's contents are displayed.

important

To view a file that is located on another computer, you usually need the program that the original file was created in loaded on the computer that you want to view it on. For example, to view a shared Microsoft Excel file on your computer, you must have Excel installed on your computer. There are some exceptions, however. For example, with Microsoft WordPad, which comes with Windows, you can view Microsoft Word files even if you do not have Word installed.

3   Double-click the file you want to view, and if prompted, type the sharing password for the other computer, and then click OK.

The program that the file was created in opens, and the file is displayed.

tip

To view files on the server computer from the client computer, on the client computer, double-click Network Neighborhood or My Network Places, and then double-click the icon representing your client computer.

4   Quit the program.

5   On the server computer, double-click My Network Places. On the Standard Buttons toolbar, click Folders, and then in the Folders list, expand Entire Network.

The contents of the My Network Places folder are displayed in the Folders list.

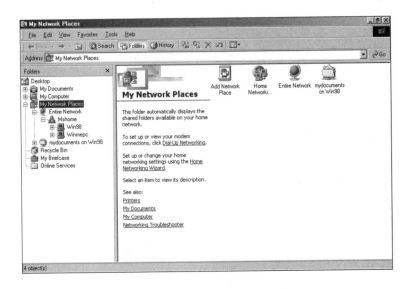

6   In the Folders list, expand My Computer, and then expand Local Disk.

The contents of the Local Disk drive are displayed. The Windows Me SBS folder is visible.

7   In the Folder window, select a file located on the other computer that you want to copy, and then drag it to the Windows Me SBS folder in the Folders list.

The File is copied to the Windows Me SBS folder.

Connecting to the Internet from a Networked Computer

Once home networking and ICS are set up on your linked computers, you can connect to the Internet from them. The process for connecting is similar to using a direct Internet connection: you can connect from your browser or e-mail program.

When you set up ICS on your home network, the computer that has the Internet connection is called the *host computer*. The computers that share that connection are called *ICS clients*.

In this exercise, your spouse wants to search the Internet for information on over-the-counter cold medication. You show your spouse how to connect to the Internet from your older computer because you're currently using your new computer for other tasks.

If you must type a password to connect to the Internet, you will be prompted to do so before the connection is made.

1   On your ICS client computer—the computer running Windows 98 in this scenario—start your Web browser.

important

If you have not previously set up an Internet connection on the client computer, the Internet Connection Wizard will appear.

Your browser connects to the Internet using the ICS host computer's Internet connection.

Internet Connection Sharing

2   On the ICS host computer, double-click the Internet Connection Sharing icon on the System Tray.

A message indicating that one computer is connected to the Internet is displayed.

3   On the ICS client computer, quit the browser.

4   On the ICS host computer, right-click the Microsoft Internet Connection Sharing icon, click Disable Internet Connection Sharing, and then click Yes to disconnect from the Internet.

The Internet connection ends.

Using Dial-Up Networking to Connect Two Computers Through Modems

For more information on creating dial-up connections, see Lesson 2, "Setting Up Internet Accounts and E-mail." For more information on shared folders, see "Sharing Folders" earlier in this lesson.

Another method of connecting two computers, similar to but more limited than home networking, is to call another computer using a dial-up connection. Both computers must have modems and be connected to separate phone lines. On the computer you want to call, you must set up the **Dial-Up Server** and enable shared folders. On the computer you call from, you need to create a dial-up connection to call the other computer. Once you have established the connection, you **map** a network drive to the computer you have connected to so that you can see shared resources on that computer.

Compared to home networks, there are some disadvantages to connecting computers through modems. First, you need two separate telephone lines. Second, communication is one-way. You can see shared resources on the computer you have dialed, but that computer cannot see resources on your computer. Finally, since the connection is through a modem, it might be too slow to make copying large files between computers practical. However, the Dial-Up Server can be useful in some situations. For example, you can set up the Dial-Up Server on your computer at home and then dial it from your computer at work to view or retrieve files.

When you set up the Dial-Up Server, make sure that you control access to the computer with a password. Otherwise, anyone who knows your phone number can call your computer and access shared resources. You might also want to keep the Dial-Up Server idle if you are not expecting anyone to call into it.

If the Dial-Up Server is not installed on your computer, you will need to install it. For help installing Windows components, see Appendix B, "Installing Microsoft Windows Me."

tip

You can also set up Dial-Up Networking to dial a network server, which will allow you to use shared network resources. For example, you might be able to dial a network server at your office and use resources on the office network. For more information on dialing network servers, see Lesson 4, "Using Windows for Work and Play."

(continued)

continued

Setting Up the Dial-Up Server

1   Open Control Panel, and then double-click the Dial-Up Networking icon.

2   On the Connections menu, click Dial-Up Server.

3   Click Allow Caller Access, and then click Apply to change the status from Idle to Monitoring.

You can double-click the Dial-Up Server icon to access the Dial-Up Server dialog box.

4   Click Change Password, enter a password to access the Dial-Up Server, and then click OK. The Dial-Up Server icon is added to the taskbar.

Connecting to the Dial-Up Server

1   On the computer you will call from, set up a dial-up connection to dial the phone number of the computer on which you have installed the Dial-Up Server.

2   To connect, double-click the Dial-Up Connection icon.

3   When the User Log On dialog box appears, type your password.

Viewing Shared Resources on the Dial-Up Server

If you are dialing in from a computer running Microsoft Windows 98, you will need to map the network drive from Windows Explorer.

1   Open My Computer, and then on the Tools menu, click Map Network Drive.

tip

You can find your computer's name in the Network dialog box in Control Panel. In Control Panel, double-click the Network icon and then click the Identification tab.

2   In the Map Network Drive dialog box, type the path for your computer in the format \\computername\foldername, and then click OK. A dialog box appears that displays all folders that you have shared on the Dial-Up Server computer.

3   Once you have finished viewing files, disconnect your computer from the Dial-Up Server.

Lesson Wrap-Up

In Lesson 3, you learned how to share folders so that folder content can be accessed over a network. Then, you set up a direct cable connection and used the connection to transfer files between two computers. You also set up a home network and viewed and copied files over the network. Finally, you shared an Internet connection to allow other computers on your home network to use the connection to access the Internet.

If you are continuing to the next lesson:

1   Close any open windows before continuing.

2   Delete the Amy.jpg file from the guest/client computer's desktop.

3   If you want to turn off File Sharing, in Control Panel, click the Network icon, click File And Print Sharing, clear the I Want To Be Able To Give Others Access To My Files check box, and then click OK twice. Repeat this step on your other computer.

4   If you want to uninstall Direct Cable Connection, in Control Panel, double-click the Add/Remove Programs icon, and then click the Windows Setup tab, click Communications, click Details, and then clear the Direct Cable Connec-tion check box. Click OK twice. Repeat this step on your other computer.

5   If you want to stop using your home network, disconnect the network cable. Repeat this step on your other computer.

6   If you want to uninstall ICS, in Control Panel, click the Add/Remove Programs icon, and then click the Windows Setup tab, click Internet Tools, click Details, and then clear the Internet Connection Sharing check box. Click OK twice. Repeat this step on your other computer.

If you are not continuing to other lessons:

1   Follow the steps in the previous section for removing items installed in this lesson.

2   If you are finished using your computer for now, log off Windows.

3   If you will not be using your computer for a long time, shut down Windows.

Glossary

client A network computer that gains access to network resources through another computer, called a server. See *server*.

Dial-Up Server A server you specify that is accessed through a public telephone service.

guest The secondary computer in Direct Cable Connection setup that accesses resources on the host computer. See *host*.

host The main computer in a Direct Cable Connection setup or Internet Connection Sharing. See *client*.

hub A device that joins communication lines at a central location to provide a central connection to all devices on a network.

map To assign a drive letter to a folder or to a computer on a network.

network A group of computers and associated devices, like printers, that are connected by cable, telephone line, or other means.

network adapter A hardware device, much like a circuit board, that connects a computer to a network. Typically, network adapters are plugged into a slot in the interior of a computer. A network cable is then plugged into a telephone jack on the adapter. Some home networking kits use external network adapters, which are separate boxes connected to a serial or parallel port on the computer and sit next to the computer, rather than being installed inside it. Also called a network interface card (NIC).

network server See *server*.

parallel Refers to transmission of data in groups of bits over parallel wires. For example, when you send a file to a parallel printer, the file is sent as simultaneous groups of bits over separate parallel wires. Most computers have parallel ports, or connectors, located on the back of the computer. Parallel devices are connected to the parallel ports using a parallel cable. Computer printers are usually connected to a parallel port. Parallel transmission is usually faster than serial transmission. See *serial*.

permissions A level of access that a user has to shared resources. When resources are shared, permissions can be set to allow a user full or partial use of the resource—for example, read-only, read- and write-only, or read, write, and delete. In Microsoft Windows Millennium Edition, users can be given permission to use shared folders and printers.

serial Refers to transmission of data sequentially, one bit at a time. For example, when a serial modem is connected to a computer, data is sent from the computer to the modem in sequence as individual bits of data. Most computers have serial ports, or connectors, located on the back of the computer. Serial devices are connected to the serial ports using a serial cable. Computer monitors are usually connected to a serial port. Serial transmission is usually slower than parallel transmission. See *parallel*.

server A computer that controls access to a network and its resources, such as printers or modem connections. See *client*.

Quick Reference

To share folders

1   Click the Start button, point to Settings, click Control Panel, and then double-click the Network icon.

2   Click File And Print Sharing, select the I Want To Be Able To Give Others Access To My Files check box, click OK twice, and then click Yes to restart your computer.

3   Right-click the folder you want to share, click Sharing, select the options you want, and then click OK.

To set up a direct cable connection between two computers

1   On the host computer, click the Start button, point to Programs, point to Accessories, point to Communications, and then click Direct Cable Connection.

2   Work through the steps in the wizard.

3   On the guest computer, click the Start button, point to Programs, point to Accessories, point to Communications, and then click Direct Cable Connection.

4   Work through the steps in the wizard.

To use a direct cable connection to transfer files

1   On the host computer, click the Start button, point to Programs, point to Accessories, point to Communications, click Direct Cable Connection, and then click Listen.

2   On the guest computer, click the Start button, point to Programs, point to Accessories, point to Communications, click Direct Cable Connection, and then click Connect.

3   On the guest computer, type the name of the host computer, and then click OK.

4   On the guest computer, open the shared folder in the host folder, and then drag the files you want to copy from the host folder to the guest desktop or to a folder on the guest computer.

5   Close the connection on the guest and host computers.

To set up a home network and share an Internet connection

1   On the server computer, click the Start button, point to Programs, point to Accessories, point to Communications, and then click Home Networking Wizard. Click Next to view the Internet Connection screen.

2   Make sure that the A Direct Connection To My ISP Using The Following Device option is selected and that the correct dial-up networking connection is displayed, and then click Next.

3   Make sure that Yes is selected. Then, make sure that your home networking adapter is listed in the Select The Device That Connects This Computer To Your Home Network box, and then click Next.

4   Click No, and then click Next. In the Computer Name box, type a name to identify your computer, and then click Next.

5   Select the My Documents Folder And All Folders In It check box, click Password, type a password for the Shared Documents folder, click OK, and then click Next.

6   Make sure that Yes, Create A Home Networking Setup Disk is selected, click Next, insert a blank floppy disk in your floppy drive, and then click Next again.

7   Click Finish. Remove the floppy disk, and then click Yes. After your computer restarts, a message asking if you want to log on to your home network is displayed. Click Yes, and then log on to Windows.

To set up home networking and Internet Connection Sharing on another computer

1   Insert the home networking floppy disk in your other computer's floppy drive. Click the Start button, and then click Run. In the Run dialog box in the Open box, type **A:setup** and then click OK.

2   Click Next. Make sure that the A Connection To Another Computer On My Home Network That Provides Direct Access To My Internet Service Provider (ISP) option is selected, and then click Next.

3   In the Computer Names box, verify the current name or type a new computer name for this computer, and then click Next to view the Share Files And Printers screen.

4   Select the My Shared Documents Folder And All Folders In It check box, make sure that the printer you want to share is selected, click Password, type a password for the Shared Documents folder, click OK, and then click Next.

5   Click Finish to complete the home networking setup, remove the floppy disk from the floppy drive, and then click Yes to restart the computer.

6   After the computer restarts, at the Windows logon prompt, type your user name and password, and then click OK.

To view and copy files over a home network

1   Make sure that you are logged on to Windows, and then on the server computer, double-click the My Network Places icon.

2   Double-click the shared computer whose files you want to view.

3   Double-click the file you want to view, and then click OK. Quit the program.

4   On the Standard Buttons toolbar, click Folders. In the Folders list, expand My Computer, and then expand Local Disk.

5   In the Folder window, select a file located on the other computer that you want to copy, and then drag it to another folder in the Folders list.

To connect to the Internet from a networked computer

1   On your ICS client computer, start your Web browser.

2   On the ICS host computer, double-click the Internet Connection Sharing icon on the System Tray.

3   On the ICS client computer, quit the browser.

4   On the ICS host computer, right-click the Internet Connection Sharing icon, and then click Disconnect.

Using a Home Network

1

Review & Practice

**ESTIMATED
TIME
20 min.**

You will review and practice how to:

✔ *Customize the Start menu.*

✔ *Create user profiles.*

✔ *Change the appearance of folders.*

✔ *Organize files and folders.*

✔ *Create Microsoft Outlook Express identities.*

✔ *Share folders.*

✔ *Set up a direct cable connection.*

✔ *Set up a home network.*

✔ *View and copy files over a home network.*

✔ *Share an Internet connection over a home network.*

In this Review & Practice section, you have an opportunity to review how to customize the Start menu, create user profiles, and customize and organize folders. You will also create Internet connections and Outlook Express identities, share folders, access files over a direct cable connection and a home network, and then share an Internet connection on a home network.

Scenario

For additional information on copying practice files, see the "Using the Microsoft Windows Me Step by Step CD-ROM" section at the beginning of this book.

Your neighbor just purchased a new computer that came with Microsoft Windows Millennium Edition pre-installed. She will use the new computer to supplement her family's other computer, which runs Microsoft Windows 98. She has asked you to show her how to use some of the important Windows Me features.

- Set up user profiles
- Use the Customize This Folder Wizard
- Organize folders
- Set up a home network to share resources

Practice files for the lesson To complete the exercises in the Review & Practice, you will need to use the Windows Me SBS folder and the following folders and the files they contain: Kid's Files and Chore List. Before you can work with any of these exercise files, you must copy them from the Microsoft Windows Me Step by Step CD-ROM to your hard disk.

Step 1:   Add a Program to the Start Menu

1   Open Control Panel.

2   Drag the Display icon to the Start button. Do not release the mouse button.

3   When the Start menu appears, drop the Display icon in the empty space at the top of the menu. When you are asked if you want to create a shortcut, click Yes.

4   Close Control Panel.

For more information about	See
Customizing the Start menu	Lesson 1

Step 2:   Set Up a User Profile

1   Open Control Panel, and then double-click the Users icon.

2   Click New User, and then work through the Add User Wizard. For your neighbor's user name, type **Heidi**; for a password, type **HE** and then in the Personalized Items Settings window, verify that none of the items are selected. Click the Create New Items To Save Disk Space option.

3   Log off, and then log back on using the Heidi profile.

For more information about	See
Setting up Windows for multiple users and creating additional user profiles	Lesson 1

Step 3: Customize Folders

1 Double-click the My Computer icon, double-click the Local Disk icon, and then double-click the Windows Me SBS folder.

2 Double-click the Chore List folder.

3 Change the folder template to the HTML Classic template by clicking the View menu, and working through the Customize This Folder Wizard.

4 Close the Chore List folder.

For more information about	See
Customizing folder appearance	Lesson 1

Step 4: Organize Folders

1 Create a new folder in the Windows Me SBS folder called Vacation Plans.

2 Find a file on your computer with the word *Vacation* in it. The file has the extension .doc.

3 In the Search Results folder, open the Folders list, and then copy the file listed in the Search pane to the Vacation Plans folder.

4 Right-click the Vacation Plans folder, point to Send To, and then click Compressed Folder.

5 Delete the original Vacation Plans folder.

For more information about	See
Using the Folders list to move and copy files and folders	Lesson 1
Using compressed folders to save disk space	Lesson 1
Using Search to find files	Lesson 1

Step 5:   Create Identities in Outlook Express

1   In Outlook Express, on the File menu, point to Identities, and then click Add New Identity.

2   Type your neighbor's name, and then select the Require A Password check box.

3   Type a new password, press Tab, type the password again, and then click OK twice.

4   Click Yes, and then work through the steps in the Internet Connection Wizard.

5   After finishing the steps in the wizard, click No when a message asking if you want to go online is displayed.

For more information about	See
Setting up Outlook Express for multiple users	Lesson 2

Step 6:   Share Folders

1   Click the Start button, point to Settings, and then click Control Panel.

2   Double-click the Network icon, and then click File And Print Sharing.

3   Select the I Want To Be Able To Give Others Access To My Files check box, and then click OK twice.

4   Click Yes.

5   Close Control Panel. Double-click the My Computer icon, double-click the Local Disk icon, and then double-click the Windows Me SBS folder.

6   Right-click the Kid's Files folder, and then click Sharing.

7   Click Shared As, click Full, and then click OK.

For more information about	See
Sharing folders	Lesson 3

Step 7:   Set Up a Direct Cable Connection

1   Click the Start button, point to Programs, point to Accessories, point to Communications, and then click Direct Cable Connection.

2   Select Host, and then click Next.

3   Click the port you want to use, connect the cable to both computers, and then click Next.

4   Click Finish, and then click Close.

5   On the guest computer, click the Start button, point to Programs, point to Accessories, point to Communications, and then click Direct Cable Connection.

6   Select Guest, and then click Next.

7   Click the port you want to use, and then click Next.

8   Click Finish, and then click Close.

For more information about	See
Setting up a direct cable connection between two computers	Lesson 3

Step 8:   Set Up a Home Network

1   On the computer that will be the server, click the Start button, point to Programs, point to Accessories, point to Communications, and then click Home Networking Wizard. Click Next.

2   Click Next, and then work through the steps in the wizard. Make sure to click the Yes, Create A Home Networking Setup Disk option in the Home Networking Setup Disk screen.

3   Remove the floppy disk, and then click Yes.

4   Without closing the Home Networking Wizard, take the setup disk and insert it into the floppy drive of the client computer you want to set up on the network.

5   On the client computer, click the Start button, click Run, and then type **a:setup** where a: is the letter of your floppy drive, and then click OK.

6   Click Next, and then work through the steps in the wizard.

7   Click Yes when prompted to restart your computer, and then at the Windows Log On prompt, click OK.

For more information about	See
Setting up a home network and sharing an Internet connection	Lesson 3
Setting up a home network and Internet Connection Sharing on another computer	Lesson 3

Step 9:   View and Copy Files over a Home Network

1   Make sure that you are logged on to Windows, and then on the client computer, double-click Network Neighborhood.

2   Double-click the shared computer whose files you want to view.

3   Double-click the file you want to view. If prompted, type the sharing password for the server computer, click OK, and then quit the program.

4   On the server computer, on the Standard Buttons toolbar, click Folders.

5   In the Folders list, expand My Computer, and then expand Local Disk.

6   In the Folder window, select a file on the client computer that you want to copy, and then drag it to the Windows Me SBS folder in the Folders list.

For more information about	See
Viewing and copying files over a home network	Lesson 3

Step 10:   Share an Internet Connection on a Home Network

1   On the ICS client computer, start your Web browser.

2   On the server computer, double-click the Microsoft Internet Connection Sharing icon on the System Tray.

For more information about	See
Connecting to the Internet from a networked computer	Lesson 3

If you are continuing to the next lesson

1   Close all open folders.

2   To delete the user profile you added during the Review & Practice, open Control Panel, double-click the Users icon, select the user profile name, and then click Delete.

3   To delete the Microsoft Outlook Express identity you created during the Review & Practice, open Outlook Express, and log off the identity you want to delete. On the File menu, point to Identities, click Manage Identities, select the identity you want to delete, and then click Remove.

4   To stop sharing the folder you shared during the Review & Practice, right-click the shared folder, click Sharing, and then click Not Shared.

5   If you want to uninstall Direct Cable Connection, in Control Panel, double-click the Add/Remove Programs icon, and then click the Windows Setup tab, click Communications, click Details, and then clear the Direct Cable Connection check box. Click OK twice. Repeat this step on your other computer.

6   If you want to stop using your home network, disconnect the network cable. Repeat this step on your other computer.

7   If you want to uninstall ICS, in Control Panel, click the Add/Remove Programs icon, and then click the Windows Setup tab, click Internet Tools, click Details, and then clear the Internet Connection Sharing check box. Click OK twice. Repeat this step on your other computer.

If you are not continuing to other lessons

1   Undo the changes you made during the Review & Practice by following steps 2 through 7 in the previous section.

2   If you are finished using your computer for now, log off Windows.

3   If you will not be using your computer for a long time, shut down Windows.

PART 2

Using Microsoft Windows Me for Home and Work Tasks

4

Using Windows for Work and Play

**ESTIMATED
TIME
20 min.**

After completing this lesson, you will be able to:

✔ *Set up speed-dial numbers to dial from Microsoft Windows Millennium Edition.*

✔ *Set dialing properties to handle certain area codes and prefixes.*

✔ *Use a calling card to make long-distance calls from Windows.*

✔ *Use the Address Book to keep track of contacts.*

✔ *Keep files synchronized when moving them between computers.*

✔ *Update files that you have transferred between computers.*

✔ *Set up a game controller.*

A family computer usually plays a dual role in any household. It's used for entertainment, and it's used for family-related work, like tracking finances, as well as work brought home from the office.

In this lesson, you will learn how to optimize Microsoft Windows Millennium Edition for both work and play. You will set up Windows Me to work with your telephone to automate calling tasks and then set up the Address Book to keep track of contacts. You will learn how to keep files synchronized as you move them between your computer at home and your computer at work. Finally, you'll set up and calibrate a game controller.

Practice files for the lesson ▷

For additional information on copying practice files and folders, see the "Using the Microsoft Windows Me Step by Step CD-ROM" section at the beginning of this book.

To complete the exercises in the lesson, you will need to use the Windows Me SBS folder and the following files and folders it contains: Contacts and the Work Projects folder. Before you can work with any of these exercise files and folders, you must copy them from the Microsoft Windows Me Step by Step CD-ROM to your hard disk. In addition, you will need extra hardware for some of the lessons: a blank, formatted floppy disk and a game controller.

Automating Phone Dialing from Windows

If you have a home office and frequently call clients or business associates while you are working on the computer, you will find that the Microsoft Phone Dialer can make the task of dialing numbers easier and more convenient. You can dial phone numbers directly from your computer, and you can set up speed dial for people you frequently call. You can also make a shortcut for Phone Dialer on your desktop or add it to the Quick Launch bar so that you can quickly get to it as you are working. Phone Dialer also keeps a log of phone calls: who the call was made to, the phone number dialed, the date and time of the call, and the duration of the call.

To use the Phone Dialer as described in this exercise, your modem must be connected to the same phone line as your telephone.

In this exercise, you have volunteered to coordinate the annual gift-wrap sale that the parent association is conducting at your son's school. Part of your job is to gather the weekly sales reports from the six team leaders and then to enter the sales information into a spreadsheet. Since the sale continues for several weeks, you decide to set up speed dial in Phone Dialer so that you can dial each team leader from Windows and then enter the sales numbers into your spreadsheet as they are reported to you. Your first task is to set up the speed-dial numbers. You decide to enter one number to try out Phone Dialer's speed-dial capability.

1   Click the Start button, point to Programs, point to Accessories, point to Communications, and then click Phone Dialer.

The Phone Dialer window opens.

2   In the Speed Dial area, click the first blank speed-dial button.

The Program Speed Dial dialog box appears.

3   In the Name box, type **Carol** and then in the Number To Dial box, type
555-0100 and then click Save.

---

tip

If you are not dialing a speed-dial number, you can enter the name of the
person you are calling in the Active Call dialog box if you want to record that
information in the Call Log.

---

*You can also
dial the number
directly from
the Phone
Dialer number
pad.*

4   Pick up your telephone receiver, and then click the Carol speed-dial button.

The call is placed. The Call Status dialog box appears, indicating the status
of the call. Because the call is not to a real number, you will hear a recorded
message, a series of clicks, or other indication that the number is not working.

5   Click Hang Up, and then hang up the telephone receiver.

---

tip

If you have a modem with voice capability, a microphone and computer speakers, or a headset, you can use the microphone and speakers to communicate
with the person you are calling instead of the telephone. This option can be
particularly useful if a telephone is not convenient or your computer doesn't use
the same phone line that your telephone uses. Check your modem documentation to see if it includes the required voice capability.

To edit a speed-dial number, on the Edit menu, click Speed Dial.

6   On the Tools menu, click Show Log.

The Call Log appears and displays a record of the call to Carol.

7   Click the Close button to close the Call Log.

Close

Creating an Area Code Rule in Phone Dialer

If you live within an area code zone that includes a large geographical area, some of the numbers you call within your area code might be long distance, requiring you to dial a "1" before dialing the number. If you live in a densely populated area, there might be many area codes within a small geographical area, and calling some of them might not require you to dial a "1" first. Remembering when you need to dial a "1" and when you don't can be confusing, so in Microsoft Phone Dialer, you can create area code rules that specify when certain prefixes need to be dialed from your location.

When you set up an area code rule in the Area Code Rules dialog box, you have the following options.

Rule	Action
When Calling Within My Area Code Always Dial The Area Code (10-Digit Dialing)	Phone Dialer adds your area code to any number you call unless you specify another area code. For example, if your area code is 999 and you dial 555-0110, Phone Dialer would dial 999-555-0110.
When Calling Within My Area Code Dial 1 For The Numbers With The Following Prefixes	When you specify a prefix, Phone Dialer dials a "1," plus your local area code, plus the number. For example, if you enter the prefix 456, and you dial the number 555-0111 within your area code of 999, Phone Dialer would dial 1-999-555-0111.
When Calling To Other Area Codes Do Not Dial 1 For Numbers With The Following Area Codes	When you list an area code outside your area, Phone Dialer will not dial a "1" before dialing a number. For example, if you were dialing from the 999 area code and listed the area code 111, Phone Dialer would not dial a "1" before dialing the number 111-555-0112.

In this exercise, you live in the 999 area code zone, but you do not need to dial that area code for all numbers in your zone. However, some of the 999 area code numbers are long distance and therefore require that you dial the area code first. In addition, a new area code has been created within the 999 area code; when you dial numbers in the new area code, they are not long distance from your location. To simplify dialing, you decide to set up area code rules for these numbers.

1   Make sure that Phone Dialer is open, and then on the Tools menu, click Dialing Properties.

The Dialing Properties dialog box appears.

2   Click Area Code Rules to display the Area Code Rules dialog box.

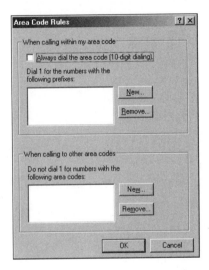

3   In the When Calling Within My Area Code area, click New, type **111** and then click OK.

The prefix 111 is added to the Dial 1 For The Numbers With The Following Prefixes list. When you call any number with the 111 prefix, Phone Dialer will prefix the number with 1-999. For example, if you set up a speed-dial number for 111-4567, Phone Dialer would dial 1-999-111-4567.

4   In the When Calling To Other Area Codes area, click New, type **222** and then click OK.

The prefix 222 is added to the Do Not Dial 1 For Numbers With The Following Area Codes list. Calls dialed to that area code will not be dialed as long-distance calls.

> **tip**
> If you dial numbers in another area code that are sometimes long distance and sometimes not, you can list that area code in the Area Code Rules dialog box as an area code that is not long distance. When you do call numbers in that area code that are long distance, you can manually add "1" to the number so that it is dialed as long distance.

5   Click OK to return to the Area Code Rules dialog box.

Setting Up Phone Dialer to Use a Calling Card

If you use a calling card to make long-distance phone calls, you can set up Microsoft Phone Dialer so that it uses the calling card in specific situations. For example, if you travel with a laptop and use your calling card when you dial in to your Internet service provider, you can have Phone Dialer dial the correct codes and numbers to use your card. Or, you might make occasional long-distance business calls from your home office. You can set up Phone Dialer to always use your business calling card for those calls.

For a demonstration of how to set up Phone Dialer to use a calling card, in the Multimedia folder on the Microsoft Windows Me Step by Step CD-ROM, double-click PhoneDialer.

To set up Phone Dialer to use a calling card in specific situations, first you need to create a new location. In Phone Dialer, a location represents a certain set of calling settings, such as always dialing your area code for local numbers. Next, you enter your calling card information. When you want to make a long-distance call using the calling card, you change to the new location and then make the call.

In this exercise, you make occasional long-distance business calls from home, and you typically use a calling card provided by your employer. You want Phone Dialer to handle these calls, so you set up location and calling card information for business calls made from home.

1   Make sure that the Dialing Properties dialog box is open, and then in the I Am Dialing From area, click New.

A message confirming that a new location was created is displayed.

The new location inherits any area code rules you have set up.

2   Click OK.

New Location is selected in the I Am Dialing From box.

3   Type **Business Calls**

The new location is renamed.

4   In the When Dialing From Here area, select the For Long Distance Calls,
        Use This Calling Card check box, and then click Calling Card.

        The Calling Card dialog box appears.

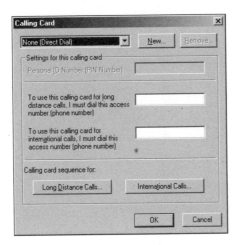

tip

Phone Dialer contains a list of companies that provide calling cards. You can
check to see if your calling card is listed by selecting the For Long Distance Calls,
Use This Calling Card check box and then examining the list. If you find your
card and select it, some of the calling card information will be entered for you.

5   Click New, type **Business Calling Card** and then click OK.

        A message explaining that you must enter rules for the calling card is dis-
        played.

6   Click OK, and then in the Personal ID Number (PIN Number) box, type
        246810

The numbers   7   In the To Use This Calling Card For Long Distance Calls, I Must Dial This
included in this   Access Number (Phone Number) box, type **10005551234** for the phone
exercise are not   number, and then click Long Distance Calls.
actual PIN or
phone numbers.   The Calling Card Sequence dialog box appears.

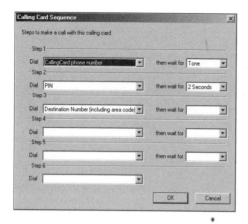

Depending on the requirements of your calling card service, you might need to adjust the Then Wait For setting to a larger or smaller number.

8   In Step 1, make sure that CallingCard Phone Number is displayed, and then in the Then Wait For box, select 8 seconds.

9   In Step 2, make sure that PIN is displayed, and then in the Then Wait For box, select 8 seconds.

10 In Step 3, make sure that Destination Number (Including Area Code) is selected, and then click OK three times to return to the Phone Dialer dialog box.

Remember to switch back to your original location before making non-business calls.

tip

Because the Business Calls location is active, any long-distance call you make will be made using your calling card. To make a call, you must enter a number into Phone Dialer and then click Dial. Phone Dialer will dial the numbers you specified in the Calling Card Sequence dialog box and then dial the destination phone number.

Using the Address Book to Keep Track of Contacts

If you use Microsoft Outlook Express as your e-mail program, you have already created contacts in the Address Book. When you reply to an e-mail message, Outlook Express adds the e-mail address to the Address Book. You can also add address information directly into the Address Book as well as import addresses from other e-mail programs or address books. When you send messages to contacts already entered in the Address Book, Outlook Express can complete the correct e-mail address as you begin typing it.

For more information about identities, see Lesson 2, "Setting Up Internet Accounts and E-mail."

If you have set up identities in Outlook Express, Address Book uses the identities to organize address information. Address Book creates a separate folder for each identity as well as a shared folder. If you reply to a message while the Charles identity is active, for example, the e-mail address is saved in the Charles folder of the Address Book. You can also share contacts among identities by copying or moving the contacts to the shared folder.

If you frequently send e-mail messages to groups of people, you can create and name a group of addresses, or distribution list, in Address Book. When you want to send e-mail messages to the group, simply type the group's name in the message To line, and Outlook Express will send the e-mail message to each person in the group.

This exercise assumes that you have set up the two identities as described in Lesson 2, "Setting Up Internet Accounts and E-mail."

In this exercise, you have a number of addresses from your old computer that you want to import to your Microsoft Windows Millennium Edition Address Book. Some of the addresses are for your spouse, so you intend to move them to the shared folder so that he can access them. Finally, you want to set up a group that consists of people on the parent-teacher association committee you are a member of.

1   Click the Start button, point to Programs, point to Accessories, and then click Address Book.

If you moved the Address Book to the Start menu in Lesson 1, you can also click Address Book on the Start menu.

     Address Book starts. The Folders list displays two folders, Shared Contacts and your contacts folder. If any contacts are in your folder, they are displayed in the Contacts list.

tip
The active identity in Address Book will be the current or last active identity in Outlook Express. For example, if the Charles identity is active in Outlook Express and you start Address Book, the Charles identity will be the active identity.

If necessary, switch to your identity. On the File menu, click Switch Identity.

2   On the File menu, point to Import, and then click Address Book (WAB).

     The Select Address Book File To Import From dialog box appears. The contents of the My Documents folder are displayed.

3   In the Look In list, click the My Computer icon.

     A list of the hard disk drives on your computer is displayed.

4   Double-click the Local Disk icon, double-click the Windows Me SBS folder, and then double-click the Contacts file.

The files are imported to Address Book. A message indicating that the import process was successful is displayed.

5   Click OK to display your list of contacts.

6   Right-click Jeff Adell, click Copy, select the Shared Contacts address book, and then on the Edit menu, click Paste.

The Jeff Adell Properties dialog box appears.

7   Click OK.

The contact is copied to the Shared Contacts address book, and the contents of the shared address book are displayed. Now, other identities will be able to view the contact information for Jeff Adell.

8   Click your folder, and then on the File menu, click New Group.

The Properties dialog box appears, and the Group tab is displayed.

To add special information about the group, click the Group Details tab.

9   In the Group Name box, type **Parent Committee**

10   Click Select Members, select Holly E. Barrett, and then click Select.

Holly E. Barrett is added to the Members list.

11   Add Martha L. Dale and Sean P. Alexander to the Members list, and then click OK twice.

The Parent Committee group is added to your contacts list. To send an e-mail message to each person listed in the group from Outlook Express, type the name of the group in the To line of your message.

Dialing Your Computer at Work

For information on using Dial-Up Networking to create an Internet connection, see Lesson 2, "Setting Up Internet Accounts and E-mail."

If your office uses a computer network, you might be able to dial directly into the network server and access shared resources on the network, such as files or e-mail. To do so, you create a dial-up connection to your computer server at work using the Make New Connection Wizard. You will need the telephone number of your server at work, plus a password, if one is required, and the name of the computer you are logging on to. You also need to make sure that you have the same **network protocol** set up on your computer as you have on the server you are dialing at work. You need to check with your system administrator at work to find out the type of protocol you need to install on your home computer. In addition, check with you system administrator to find out what resources are shared on the network and whether you can access your e-mail messages that you receive at work.

1   Click the Start button, point to Settings, and then click Dial-Up Networking.

2   Double-click Make New Connection, in the Type A Name For The Computer You Are Dialing box, type **Office Server** and then click Next.

3   Type the phone number of the computer you want to call, click Next, click Finish, and then double-click the Office Server connection.

4   Type your user name and password, and then click Connect.

5   Click Close, double-click My Network Places, and then double-click Entire Network.

Keeping Transferred Files Synchronized Using Briefcase

If you frequently transfer files between computers—such as between a laptop and your desktop computer or between your home computer and your computer at work—you might have trouble keeping track of which computer has the most recent file on it. Or, you might find it cumbersome to manually update files when transferring them.

To make the task of transferring files easier, you can use Briefcase to synchronize files that you transfer between computers. Briefcase is a feature that helps you keep track of files or folders when you transfer them between computers. When you copy a file or folder to Briefcase, a link between the two files is created. You copy Briefcase to a floppy disk, and then copy Briefcase from the floppy disk to your other computer. On the second computer, you can work on the file in Briefcase, and then when you are finished, transfer Briefcase back to your main computer and have Briefcase update the original file on your hard disk.

In this exercise, you have spent some time over the weekend working on two files that you will need to finish at work. If you don't have time to finish them at work, you'll probably take them home again to continue working on them. Because you might be transferring the files several times, you want to make it easier to keep track of them. You decide to use Briefcase to help you with that task.

If the Briefcase icon is not on the desktop, you will need to install it. For help installing Windows components, see Appendix B, "Installing Microsoft Windows Me."

1   Double-click the My Computer icon, double-click the Local Disk icon, and then double-click the Windows Me SBS folder.

2   Double-click the Work Projects folder.

3   Drag Prospective Student Letter and State University Letter to My Briefcase on the desktop.

   The files remain in the Work Projects folder, and copies of them are created in My Briefcase.

4   Double-click the My Briefcase icon.

   The files are listed in My Briefcase. Note that the location, status, and size of the original files are displayed in the Window.

If this is the first time you have started My Briefcase, the Welcome To The Windows Briefcase Help window also appears. Click Finish to exit.

5   Close My Briefcase.

6   Insert a floppy disk in your floppy drive, and then in the Work Projects folder, click Back three times to return to My Computer.

7   Drag My Briefcase to the floppy disk icon in My Computer.

   My Briefcase is moved to your floppy disk.

Close

8   Remove the floppy disk from the floppy drive, and then click the Close button on the My Computer window.

important

Your files must be small enough to fit on one floppy disk. If you want to transfer larger files, consider either compressing the files first or compressing the floppy disk. For more information on compressing files, see Lesson 1, "Customizing Windows for Personal Use." You can also use high-capacity disks or read/write CDs to transfer My Briefcase files.

tip
You can create a new briefcase on your desktop by right-clicking the desktop, pointing to New, and then clicking Briefcase. The copy will be named New Briefcase.

Updating My Briefcase Files

Once you have copied the files to My Briefcase and then copied My Briefcase to your floppy disk, you are ready to transfer them to a second computer. The best way to edit the files on your second computer is to open My Briefcase from the floppy disk and work on the files. When you are finished, you transfer the floppy disk back to your first computer and then update the original files.

If you do not use a computer at work for this exercise, you can use any other computer that is running Microsoft Windows 95, Windows 98, or Windows Me.

In this exercise, now that you have My Briefcase copied to a floppy disk, you are ready to take the files with you to work to edit them, and then bring them home again to complete the editing.

1   Insert the floppy disk from the previous exercise in the floppy drive of your work computer, double-click the My Computer icon, and then double-click the floppy disk drive icon.

The contents of the floppy disk drive, including the My Briefcase icon, are displayed.

2   Double-click the My Briefcase icon.

My Briefcase starts, and the two files are displayed.

If it is more convenient, you can move the files to any folder on your computer.

3   Drag the files from My Briefcase to the desktop.

The files are copied to the desktop.

4   Open the Prospective Student Letter, and type the following sentence at the end of the letter: **In addition, we have fully equipped studios and computer labs for our electronic design courses.** Then, save and close the letter.

5   Open the State University Letter, and type the following sentence at the end of the letter: **Our students are highly motivated and will make a definite contribution to the student body at State University.** Then, save and close the letter.

6   In My Briefcase, on the Standard Buttons toolbar, click Update All.

The Update My Briefcase dialog box appears, indicating that the My Briefcase files will be updated with the modified files on your desktop.

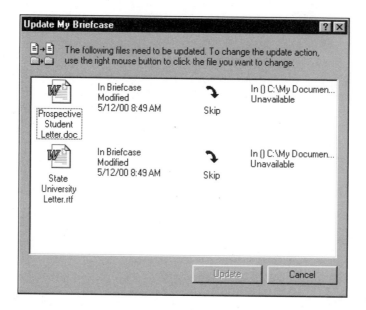

tip
Right-click the file icons in the Update My Briefcase dialog box to change the update action. You can have My Briefcase skip updating one or more of the files, or reverse the updating so that the file on the desktop is updated with the copy in My Briefcase.

7 Click Update.

When the update is complete, the My Briefcase dialog box closes.

8 Remove the floppy disk from your work computer and then insert it in the floppy drive of your home computer.

9 Double-click the My Computer icon on your home computer, and then double-click the floppy disk drive icon.

The contents of the floppy disk, including the My Briefcase icon, are displayed.

If you plan to transfer the files back to your work computer, leave My Briefcase on the floppy disk.

10 Right-click the My Briefcase icon, and then click Update All.

The Update My Briefcase dialog box appears, indicating that the My Briefcase copies will replace the original files on your hard disk.

11 Click Update.

The files on your hard disk are updated.

12 In the floppy disk drive window, click Back to return to My Computer.

13 In My Computer, double-click the Local Disk icon, double-click the Windows Me SBS folder, and then double-click the Work Projects folder.

14 Open each letter, review the contents, and then close the letters.

Each letter has been updated with the changes you made to the copies on your other computer.

15 Close the Work Projects folder.

tip

Once you have finished working on the letters on your home computer, you can update the files in My Briefcase on the floppy disk, take them back to work, and then update the copies on your work computer.

Using Briefcase with a Direct Cable Connection or Network Connection

For more information on direct cable connections and home networks, see Lesson 3, "Using a Home Network."

If you have a direct cable connection between two computers—for example, between a desktop computer and a laptop—you can use Briefcase to keep files updated.

1 Make sure that the files you want to transfer are in a shared folder.

2 Create a Briefcase folder on the second computer.

3 If you are using a direct-cable connection, connect the first computer to the second computer. If you are using a network, make sure that the network is running.

4 Copy the files from the first computer to the Briefcase folder on the second computer.

5 Edit the files in the Briefcase folder on the second computer. The computers do not need to be connected to edit the files.

6 Re-establish the connection if necessary, and then on the Standard Buttons toolbar, click Update All.

7 When the Update Briefcase dialog box appears, click Update. The files are updated on the first computer.

Using Windows for Work/Play   4

Adding and Calibrating a Game Controller

If you play action games, you will probably want to use a game controller. Although you can often play action games with keyboard commands, a game controller is usually essential if you want to take full advantage of the game's capabilities.

Game controllers come in many shapes and sizes. In Microsoft Windows Millennium Edition, you can quickly add and calibrate over 25 different types of controllers. You can also create custom controller configurations, or if you have software for a special controller, you can also install the software to configure the controller. Once you have added the controller, you can calibrate it so that it functions properly.

In this exercise, you have just purchased a 3-axis, 2-button joystick to use with your children's games, and you want to set it up on your computer to make sure that it operates correctly. You have plugged it into the game port on your computer, and now you're ready to add the controller and calibrate it.

While the exercise describes the steps for a certain joystick, the process is very similar for other types of game controllers.

1   Click the Start button, point to Settings, and then click Control Panel to display the contents of the Control Panel folder.

2   Double-click the Gaming Options icon.

The Gaming Options dialog box appears.

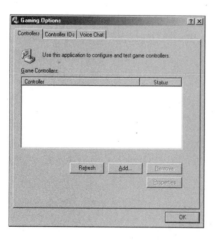

3   Click Add.

The Add Game Controller dialog box appears.

tip

To create a customized configuration, click Custom. If your controller came with its own software or is not on the Game Controllers list, click Add Other.

4   In the Game Controllers list, click 3-Axis, 2-Button Joystick, and then click OK.
The controller is added to the list. The status is listed as OK.

important

If the status in the Game Controllers list is Not Connected, you might not have your controller properly connected to your game port. Check the connection, and if the problem persists, contact your computer or game controller manufacturer.

You can add more than one controller to the Game Controllers list. However, you must connect the controller to your computer to calibrate it.

5   Click Properties, and then click the Settings tab.
The Game Controller Properties dialog box appears, and the Settings tab is displayed. Even if your controller seems to be functioning properly, it is a good idea to calibrate it right after you have installed it.

6   Click Calibrate.
The Controller Calibration dialog box appears.

7   Press one of the buttons on the controller, move the controller handle in a circle several times, and then click a controller button.

8   Click a controller button again, and then click Next.

9   Move the third axis control forward and back several times, and then press a button on the controller.
The third axis control is usually a dial or slider control on the base of the joystick. It is often used as a throttle or speed control in some action games. A message indicating that you have successfully calibrated your controller is displayed.

10   Click Finish, click OK twice, and then close Control Panel.
Your game controller has been added and calibrated.

tip

With some Internet games, you can use voice chat to communicate with other players. For details on enabling voice chat, click the Voice Chat tab in the Gaming Options dialog box, and then click Details.

Playing Internet Games

There are a number of new games that come with Microsoft Windows Millennium Edition, many of which can be played over the Internet, such as Internet Checkers, Internet Hearts, Internet Backgammon, and others. The Internet games work in conjunction with the MSN Gaming Zone, a Web site that hosts a number of Internet games. When you start an Internet game, you are connected to the MSN Gaming Zone, which in turn connects you with another player online who is looking for a partner.

For information on connecting to the Internet, see Lesson 2, "Setting Up Internet Accounts and E-mail."

You can also go directly to the MSN Gaming Zone Web site, www.zone.com, where you have an even greater choice of games. On the Web site are links to dozens of games in a number of categories—for example, action, adventure, card, and sports. The games are divided into free games and premium games. To play the premium games, you need to pay a monthly fee. For any game you want to play, you need to register first with MSN Gaming Zone. The MSN Gaming Zone Web site also has links to game chats, a game events calendar, and news about new games.

Playing a Windows Internet Game

1   Click the Start button, point to Programs, point to Games, and then click the Internet game you want to play.

2   When the MSN Gaming Zone dialog box appears, you can click Help to find out more about the game. The Frequently Asked Questions topic is a good source of general information about Internet gaming for first-time players.

3   Click Play, and then connect to the Internet. The MSN Gaming Zone searches for a partner based on your skill level, language, and location. Once a player is found, you can chat during the game. The only personal information that MSN Gaming Zone shares with other players is your skill level and language.

Choosing an Internet Game from Gaming Zone

1   Log on to the Internet, and then go to www.zone.com. The home page contains a list of popular games as well as links to game categories. You can also click Profiles to search for a specific player.

2   Before you play a game, click the Help link, and then click New Member Tutorial. The tutorial explains how game playing works and how to sign on to a game.

3 Click the Free Sign Up link to register. You must register before you can play a game.

4 To start playing a game, click one of the games on the home page, or click one of the game categories to select a game.

Lesson Wrap-Up

In Lesson 4, you learned how to use Microsoft Phone Dialer to automate phone dialing from your computer. You also learned how to import files into the Address Book as well as move contacts between folders and create groups of contacts. You set up a dial-up connection for a network server, and then used Briefcase to keep files up to date when you transferred them. You also learned how to add and calibrate a game controller.

If you are continuing to the next lesson:

1 Click the Start button, point to Programs, point to Accessories, point to Communications, and then click Phone Dialer. Delete the speed-dial number you created in this lesson.

2 In Phone Dialer, open Dialing Properties, and then delete the location you created in this lesson.

3 In Dialing Properties, click Area Code Rules, and then delete the rules you created in this lesson.

4 In Dialing Properties, click Calling Card, and then remove the calling card you set up in this lesson.

5 Click the Start button, point to Programs, point to Accessories, and then click Address Book. Delete all of the contacts added during this lesson.

6 Delete the files you placed on the desktop of your work computer in the "Updating My Briefcase" exercise.

7 Close any open windows before continuing.

If you are not continuing to other lessons:

1 Follow the steps in the previous section for deleting or removing items created in this lesson.

2 If you are finished using your computer for now, log off Windows.

3 If you will not be using your computer for a long time, shut down Windows.

Glossary

network protocol Software that defines a set of rules and parameters that enable communication through a network. Microsoft Windows Me includes network protocols for Internet connections and several protocols for networks.

Quick Reference

To automate phone dialing from Windows

1   Click the Start button, point to Programs, point to Accessories, point to Communications, and then click Phone Dialer.

2   Click a blank speed-dial button, type the name and number of the person you want to set up, and then click Save.

3   Pick up your telephone receiver, and then click the speed-dial button for the speed-dial number you just created.

4   Click Hang Up when the call is complete.

5   To view the Call Log, on the Tools menu, click Show Log.

To create an area code rule in Phone Dialer

1   Make sure that Microsoft Phone Dialer is open, and then on the Tools menu, click Dialing Properties.

2   Click Area Code Rules.

3   In the When Calling Within My Area Code section, click New, type the phone prefix, and then click OK.

4   In the When Calling To Other Area Codes section, click New, type the area code, and then click OK twice.

To set up Phone Dialer to use a calling card

1   Make sure that the Dialing Properties dialog box is open, and then next to the I Am Dialing From box, click New, type a name for the location that you are creating, and then click OK.

2   Click Calling Card, click New, type a name, and then click OK twice.

3   In the Personal ID Number (PIN Number) box, type your calling card PIN.

4   In the To Use This Calling Card For Long Distance Calls, I Must Dial This Access Number (Phone Number) box, type the calling card access number, and then click Long Distance Calls.

5   In Steps 1 through 6, make sure that the correct items are selected. Adjust the Then Wait For box as needed. Click OK twice.

To use the Address Book to keep track of contacts

1   Click the Start button, point to Programs, point to Accessories, and then click Address Book.

2   To import contacts, in the Address Book, on the File menu, point to Import, and then click Address Book (WAB). Locate and select the contact file you want to import, and then click Open.

3   To move a contact from an identity file to the shared folder, right-click the contact, click Copy, select the Shared folder, and then on the Edit menu, click Paste.

4   To create a contacts group, click New Group, type a name for the group, click Select Members, add contacts to the Members list, and then click OK twice.

To keep transferred files synchronized using Briefcase

1   Drag the file you want to transfer to My Briefcase.

2   Insert a floppy disk in your floppy drive, and then double-click the My Computer icon.

3   Drag My Briefcase to the floppy disk icon in My Computer.

To update My Briefcase files

1   Insert the floppy disk containing My Briefcase in the floppy drive of the computer you want to transfer files to, double-click the My Computer icon, and then double-click the floppy disk drive icon.

2   Double-click the My Briefcase icon, drag the file from My Briefcase to the desktop, open the transferred file, and then edit it.

3   In My Briefcase, click Update All, click Update, and when the update is complete, close the My Briefcase dialog box.

4   Remove the floppy disk from the second computer and then insert it in the floppy drive of the first computer.

5   In the My Computer folder, double-click the floppy disk icon, right-click My Briefcase, click Update All, and then click Update.

To add and calibrate a game controller

1   Click the Start button, point to Settings, click Control Panel, double-click the Gaming Options icon.

2   Click Add, in the Game Controllers list, select your game controller, and then click OK.

3   Click Properties, click the Settings tab, and then click Calibrate.

4   Press one of the buttons on the controller, move the controller handle in a circle several times, and then click a controller button.

5   Click a controller button again, and then click Next.

6   Move the third axis control forward and back several times, and then press a button on the controller.

7   Click Finish, click OK twice, and then close Control Panel.

5

Getting the Most Out of Multimedia

**ESTIMATED
TIME
45 min.**

After completing this lesson, you will be able to:

✔ *Make voice recordings and attach them to document files.*

✔ *Play music CDs and multimedia files with Microsoft Windows Media Player.*

✔ *Play radio stations that broadcast over the Internet.*

✔ *Download local TV listings from the Web and view them.*

✔ *Use Microsoft WebTV for Windows to view television programs on your computer.*

✔ *Transfer photos from a digital camera to Microsoft Windows Millennium Edition.*

✔ *Edit digital photos using Kodak Imaging for Windows.*

✔ *Crop a photo for use in a document.*

✔ *Create and edit a video clip with Microsoft Movie Maker.*

Getting the Most Out of Multimedia

Microsoft Windows Millennium Edition provides a number of programs for accessing, playing, or editing multimedia—including audio recordings, audio and visual files such as film clips, Internet radio broadcasts, television broadcasts, and **digital** photos. The programs can be used for practical purposes, such as viewing digital training films or for entertainment. You want to learn more about these programs so that you can take advantage of the multimedia content available from the Web and other sources.

In this lesson, you will learn how to record voice annotations and copy them to a document. You will play music CDs, multimedia files, and listen to radio broadcasts on the Web. You will also learn how to use Microsoft WebTV for Windows—download and search TV listings and listen to TV broadcasts. You will also download photos from your **digital camera** and then edit the photos. Finally, you will use Microsoft Movie Maker to create and edit a movie.

Practice files
for the lesson ➡

For more infor-
mation on set-
ting up an
Internet con-
nection, see
Lesson 2, "Set-
ting Up
Internet Ac-
counts and E-
mail."

For additional
information on
copying prac-
tice files, see
the "Using the
Microsoft
Windows Me
Step by Step
CD-ROM"
section at the
beginning of
this book.

To complete the exercises in the lesson, you will need to use the Windows Me SBS folder and the following files that it contains: Waterfall and Annual Budget. You will also need the Movie folder. Before you can work with any of these exercise files, you must copy them from the Microsoft Windows Me Step by Step CD-ROM to your hard disk. For some of the exercises in this lesson, you will need to have an Internet connection set up on your computer. You will also need special hardware: a sound card; a microphone and speakers or headphones for recording and listening to voice files; a TV tuner card and antenna or cable connection to receive television programs; and a digital camera that has photos stored in memory to use the Windows photo transfer program. You will also need a music CD to use Microsoft Windows Media Player.

Recording Voice Messages

When you review a document, instead of scribbling comments on it or typing your comments online, you can use Microsoft Sound Recorder to record comments and insert them or link them to the document that you are reviewing.

For information
on modifying
and mixing
sounds, see
Sound Recorder
Help.

Of course, there are other uses for Sound Recorder. For instance, you can record a greeting and then place it in your Windows Startup folder so that the greeting plays whenever Microsoft Windows Millennium Edition starts. You can make your Windows desktop a voice message center. If you plan to not be home when your kids return from school, you can record a message for them and place it on the desktop so that they can play it when they get home.

To record a message or greeting with Sound Recorder, you click the Record button and then record the message. To play the message back, you click the Play button. You can add an echo effect to your recording, speed it up, slow it down, or play it in reverse. You can also combine sound files and mix sound files. To record a message or greeting, you need a microphone; to play it back, you need speakers or headphones. You also need a sound card capable of working with Sound Recorder.

In this exercise, you need to review a draft of the annual budget your spouse has prepared. Rather than writing comments, you decide to record voice comments and then place them in the document so that your spouse can review them later.

1 On the desktop, double-click the My Computer icon, double-click the Local Disk icon, and then double-click the Windows Me SBS folder. Double-click the Annual Budget file.

2 Click the Start button, point to Programs, point to Accessories, point to Entertainment, and then click Sound Recorder.

Sound Recorder starts.

Record

3 Click the Record button, and then record this message into the microphone: **I think we need to cut our housing expenses this year. What do you think about refinancing?** Click the Stop button to stop recording.

Stop

4 Click the Play button to play back your message.

Play

> **tip**
> To adjust the playback volume from the Sound Recorder, click Effects, and then click Increase Volume or Decrease Volume. To adjust the recording volume, click the Start button, point to Programs, point to Accessories, point to Entertainment, and then click Volume Control. On the Options menu, click Properties, select Recording, and then make sure that Microphone is selected. Click OK, and then adjust the Microphone Balance control.

> **tip**
> You can delete part of a recording by positioning the slider just before or just after the portion of the message you want to delete, and then on the Edit menu clicking Delete Before Current Position or Delete After Current Position. To add to a recording, move the slider to the point in the recording where you want to record, and then begin recording.

Multimedia

5   On the Sound Recorder File menu, click Save. On the desktop, click the My Computer icon, double-click Local Disk, and then double-click the Windows Me SBS folder.

The Windows Me SBS folder opens.

6   In the File Name box, type **Housing** and then click Save.

7   On the Sound Recorder File menu, click New.

8   Click the Record button, and then record this message: **Let's talk to our accountant about reducing taxes this year.**

9   On the File menu, click Save. In the File Name box, type **Taxes** and then click Save.

10   Quit Sound Recorder, right-click the taskbar, and then click Tile Windows Vertically.

11   In the Windows Me SBS folder, right-click the Housing file, and then click Copy.

12   In the Annual Budget file, click after $8200 in the Housing row, and then on the Edit menu, click Paste.

The sound message is copied to the Annual Budget file.

13   In the Windows Me SBS folder, right-click the Taxes file, and then click Copy.

14   In the Annual Budget file, click after $7000 in the Taxes row, and then on the Edit menu, click Paste.

The sound message is copied to the Annual Budget file.

15   In the Annual Budget file, double-click the first sound icon to play the message.

16   Double-click the second sound icon to play the message.

tip
You can change the position of the sound icon by dragging it to a new location.

17   Close the Windows Me SBS folder, and then close the Annual Budget file. Click Yes when you are prompted to save the file.

Understanding Windows Media Player

With Microsoft Windows Media Player, you can play just about any media **file format**, including audio, video, and multimedia files. In fact, Media Player is the heart of Windows multimedia—you can play and copy CD tracks to your computer, create a library of multimedia files, create playlists of music selections, play **streaming** media from the Web, and copy music to a portable device.

When you use Media Player, it's easy to locate the feature you want—each feature is represented by a button on the main Media Player screen. In addition, the volume control and other controls are within easy reach.

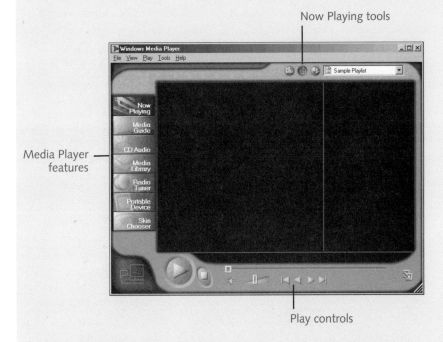

Media Player features — (label pointing to left-side buttons)

Now Playing tools

Play controls

See the exercises later in this lesson for more information about playing music CDs, multimedia files, and listening to Web radio stations.

You'll probably use Media Player mainly for playing music CDs, viewing multimedia files, and listening to Web radio. But Media Player has two features that will help you find and organize multimedia content: the Media Guide and the Media Library. In addition, the Media Player has added **skins** and **visualizations**, which you can use to personalize and enhance the use of multimedia files.

(continued)

continued

Media Player

To start Media Player, click the Media Player icon on the Quick Launch bar. You can switch Media Player between Full Mode or Compact Mode by choosing Full or Compact Mode on the View menu. In Full Mode, you can use all of the Media Player features; in Compact Mode, fewer features are available.

Using the Media Library to Organize Your Multimedia Files

In the Media Library, you can create and organize playlists—lists of multimedia files that you want to keep track of and return to later. The Media Library is similar to the Favorites list in Microsoft Internet Explorer, but in the Media Library, you have more flexibility about how you organize the items you enter. To add a file to a playlist, you must first add it to a Media Library category—Audio, Video, or Radio Tuner Presets. Then, you can transfer the item to a specific playlist in the Media Library. See the Organizing Your Media Collection topic in Media Player Help for more information on using the Media Library.

Transferring Multimedia Files to a Portable Device

You might want to transfer multimedia files—or an entire playlist—from your desktop computer to another device, such as a palm-size computer or a laptop. To use the Microsoft Windows Media Player Transfer feature, you first copy the files to Media Player. Next, you connect the two devices with a cable attached to communication ports on each device. Then, click Portable Device in Media Player. In the Portable Device window, you can select individual files or entire playlists, and then transfer them to your portable device. You can only transfer certain file types, and in the case of commercially produced music or videos, you need to be aware of the copyright and licensing restrictions. See Media Player Help for more on transferring files. For specific information on licensing, see the Copying Music To Your Portable Device topic in Media Player Help.

Understanding Skins and Visualizations

Microsoft Windows Media Player includes two new features that you might find make playing multimedia files more interesting: skins and visualizations. A *skin* is a customized version of Media Player and is only available in Compact Mode. Skins present a new look and feel to the Media Player. To try out a new skin, click Skin Chooser.

Visualizations are splashes of color or shapes that appear while an audio file is playing, similar to some Windows screen savers. To view a visualization, make sure that an audio file is playing, and then click Now Playing in Media Player. You can switch visualizations by clicking the arrows in the lower-left corner of the screen. You can also download additional visualizations from the Internet by clicking Download Visualizations on the Tools menu in Microsoft Internet Explorer.

For more information on skins and visualizations, see the Customizing Windows Media Player topic in Media Player Help.

Playing Music CDs

For a demonstration of how to play a music CD, in the Multimedia folder on the Microsoft Windows Me Step by Step CD-ROM, double-click MediaPlayer.

If you don't have a stereo system or your stereo system is not located in the same room as your computer, you can still play your favorite music while you use the computer. With Microsoft Windows Media Player, you can play CDs in your computer's CD-ROM drive, even while you are working on the same computer. You can control how the CDs play, switch tracks, copy tracks to a playlist in the Media Library, and even connect to the Internet to get information about the CD or the CD artist. In fact, Media Player gives you more control over how CDs play than many stereo-system CD players.

In this exercise, you've run across a forgotten CD in your collection. You decide to use Media Player to play it and copy a track to the Media Library.

Media Player

1   On the Quick Launch bar, click the Media Player icon.

Media Player starts.

To adjust the volume, move the Volume control in the lower area of the Media Player frame.

2   Insert a music CD in your CD-ROM drive, and then click CD Audio.

After a few moments, a list of the CD tracks and other information appears on the CD Audio screen, and the CD begins playing. The currently playing track is highlighted.

For more information, see "Using the Internet to Find Information About Music CDs" later in this lesson.

tip

If you are currently connected to the Internet, the CD artist and track names are available from the Internet and will display on the CD Audio screen. If you are not connected to the Internet or the information is not available, you will see generic track names; the artist and genre will not be listed.

Checkmark

3   Click the Checkmark icon at the top of the first column to clear all of the track check boxes, and then select a check box next to a track that you want to copy.

The Checkmark icon can be used to select or clear all of the tracks on a CD.

4   Click Copy Music.

The track is copied to the Media Library. The Copy Status column indicates the copy progress. The message "Copied to Library" displays in the Copy Status column when the copying is complete.

5   Click the Pause button, and then click Media Library.

Pause

The Media Library opens, and the Audio category is expanded in the left pane. The left pane displays the subcategories for audio CDs as well as categories for video media and other items. The right pane displays the track that you have copied from the CD.

If you have a license, a license to use the copied music is also transferred to your computer.

6   Click New Playlist, and then in the New Playlist dialog box, type **My Favorite Songs** and then click OK.

7   Select the track that you copied, click Add To Playlist, and then click Add To My Favorite Songs.

8   Remove the CD from the CD-ROM drive. In My Playlists, click My Favorite Songs, select the track you copied, and then click the Play button.

Play

The track plays.

9   Click Now Playing.

A visualization is displayed in the Now Playing screen.

tip
You can change visualizations by clicking the Next Visualization button on the Now Playing screen.

Stop

10   Click the Stop button.

tip
You can change CD Audio options and options for other Media Player features on the Tools menu by clicking Options, and then clicking the appropriate tab. For example, you can also adjust the copying quality in the CD Audio tab by adjusting the slider in the Copying Settings area.

Using the Internet to Find Information About Music CDs

When you play a CD in Microsoft Windows Media Player, you can sometimes download the CD playlist and other CD information from the Internet. But you can also find more information about the CD, such as reviews of the CD or biographical information about the artist from the Internet. You can connect to or search for this information from Media Player, even while you are playing a CD.

Searching the Internet for the CD Playlist

This exercise follows steps for playing a CD by a particular artist. Steps may slightly differ if you play a soundtrack or compilation CD.

1   Make sure that the CD Audio screen is displayed and that a music CD is in the CD-ROM drive.

2   Click Get Names. When prompted, connect to the Internet. The WindowsMedia.com Ready To Search screen appears.

3   Click Next, click Yes, and in the Search For Artist box, type the artist name, and then click Next.

4   In the Choose Artist screen, select the artist name, and then click Next.

5   In the Choose Album screen, select the album name, click Next, and then in the Save Track Information screen, click Finish to add the information to your library.

(continued)

Multimedia

5

continued

6 If the CD information is not available, make sure that the CD Audio screen is open and that a music CD is in. In the Enter Track Information screen, type the track information manually, and then click Finish to add the information to your library.

Searching the Internet for information about the CD artists

1 Make sure that the CD Audio screen is open and that a music CD is in the CD-ROM drive.

2 Click Album Details, and then make sure that you are connected to the Internet. The WindowsMedia.com Web page opens in Media Player. If information about the album is available, it is displayed.

3 To find additional information, click Artist Profile.

Upgrading to DVD

MILLENNIUM New!

Digital video disc (DVD) is a relatively new technology that is sometimes referred to as the next-generation CD. DVDs look very much like CDs but hold much more data—between 4.7 and 8.5 gigabytes (GB), compared with 650 megabyte (MB) on a CD. Double-sided DVDs can hold 17 GB. *Digital* means that data is stored as a series of numbers (1s and 0s) on the disk, which makes it possible to pack more on the disk as well as to attain higher quality playback.

To use a DVD, you need a DVD drive, plus any associated hardware, and a DVD player. A DVD player is similar to a CD player; you use it to control the playing of a DVD. Microsoft Windows Millennium Edition includes a DVD player, and often DVD drives come with their own player. DVD doesn't mean that you have to give up your CDs—you can play both with a DVD player.

A common application for DVD is movies. You can store several feature-length movies on a single DVD, and you can search for special features, such as movie trailers and character biographies. And, if you want to find that special scene in your favorite movie, you don't have to fast-forward to find it. In addition, the quality of DVD video and audio playback is much better than that of videotape.

To use the DVD player, make sure that your DVD hardware is installed and configured according to the manufacturer's instructions. To start the DVD, insert the DVD in the DVD drive. You can also click DVD Player on the Start/Programs/Accessories/Entertainment menu. DVD movies are usually divided into sections, and you can search for the section you are interested in. For more information on DVD Player, search for the DVD topic in Windows Help and consult the DVD Player documentation.

Playing Multimedia Files

If you equate multimedia with training films, you might be missing out on the rich collection of multimedia available on the Web. Using Microsoft Windows Media Player to play those multimedia files—as well as training presentations—is easy. If the file is on your hard disk or a CD, you simply open the file in Media Player, and the file plays automatically. You can adjust the volume; start, pause, and stop the clip; and fast-forward or rewind the video clip.

To view multimedia files over the Internet, you load the files directly into Media Player from a Web site or save a shortcut to the file in Media Library to play the file later. When you play a file from a Web page, the video and audio is streamed to Media Player. Depending on your modem connection speed, the file might halt for a few seconds while playing as Media Player processes the incoming file. When that happens, the word *buffering* will appear on the lower portion of the Media Player screen.

In this exercise, you are intrigued with idea of viewing audio-video Web content, such as newscasts, educational information, and entertainment such as music videos. You decide to use Media Player to investigate the kind of content available to you.

If you are not connected to the Internet, log on when you are prompted.

1   Make sure that Media Player is open, and then click Media Guide.

The WindowsMedia.com Web site opens. The Web site contains tabs for a Home page, a Music page, a Radio page, and a **Broadband** page.

important

Most broadband links are meant to be used by high-speed Internet connections. If your modem operates at 28.8 kilobits per second (Kbps) or 56 Kbps, scroll down in the Media Guide screen to browse additional broadband links. You can often locate content that will play at 28.8 Kbps and 56 Kbps. For example, click the Music tab and select a video compatible with your connection speed.

2   Click the Music tab, and then click a video link.

A message appears on the lower portion of the Media Guide screen indicating that Media Player is **buffering**, meaning that a small part of the file content is being streamed to your computer and stored temporarily before playing. After a few moments, the video and audio content begins to play.

3   On the View menu, point to Zoom, and then click Fit To Window.

important

Video quality and download time depends in part on the speed at which your modem operates. At the speeds that standard modems usually operate, 28.8 Kbps to 56 Kbps, video quality tends to be fair to poor.

4   To select a new skin, click Skin Chooser. In the Skin Chooser list, click Headspace, and then click Apply Skin.

The new skin is applied while the video is still playing.

Click the arrow on the right ear to display the current playlist.

5   Click the arrow on the left ear to view the graphic equalizer, move the Volume slider to adjust the volume to your liking, and then click the arrow on the left ear to close the controls.

You will have a different video playing on the Skin screen.

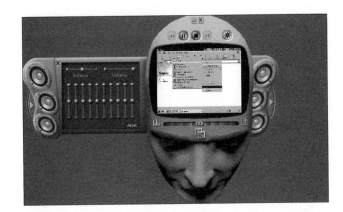

Return To Full Mode

6   Click the Return To Full Mode button that is located in the middle of the Headspace skin, and then click Now Playing.

tip

When the Media Player is in Compact Mode, a small window appears in the lower-right corner of the screen displaying the Return To Full Mode button. You can click the window for more options, such as returning to Full Mode or selecting a new skin.

7   On the File menu, click Close.
The video clip stops playing.

Listening to Web Radio

Unless you have a short-wave radio, your listening to radio broadcasts is probably restricted to those local stations your radio can pick up or to those your cable company offers. However, with Microsoft Windows Media Player, you can receive many national and international stations that broadcast on the Internet. For example, you can listen to stations in New York and Los Angeles or in France, Great Britain, Greece, and in many other countries.

Unlike playing multimedia files, Media Player does not provide video content to accompany radio broadcasts, but it does display information about the broadcast, and you can make adjustments to volume and other settings. To listen to Web radio, you connect to the Internet from Media Player and then choose the station that you want to listen to. Media Player includes a link to the Microsoft Windows Media Web site from which you can select radio stations. The Web site includes featured stations, and you can find additional stations that broadcast on the Internet, both in the United States and abroad. You can search by keyword or by category. You can also connect to international radio guides that provide more information about stations in various countries.

In this exercise, you want to listen to a radio station while you are working, so you decide to use Media Player to search for one of your liking.

If you are not connected to the Internet, log on when you are prompted.

1   Make sure that Media Player is open, and then click Radio Tuner.

2   In the Station Finder pane, click the Find By down arrow, and then click Format. In the Select Format box, click the down arrow, and then click Classical.

If your Web browser appears, minimize it.

3   In the Station Name list, double-click a station to listen to a broadcast.

The broadcast plays. Status information about the broadcast appears above the Media Player controls. Information about the station appears at the top of the Media Player.

tip

Point to a station name in the Station Finder list to view details about the station. To view more information in the Station Finder or Presets panes, maximize the Media Player window, and then adjust the panes by dragging the center border. You can also sort stations in the Station Finder by clicking a header bar in the Station Finder list.

4   In the Presets pane, click the Featured down arrow, and then click My Presets.

You can have up to 12 stations in a preset list.

5   Click Add.

The currently playing station is added to the My Presets list.

6   In the Station Finder pane, click Search.

The Advanced Station Search—Web Page Dialog box appears.

7   Click the Language down arrow, and then click English. Click the Country (Region) down arrow, click United Kingdom, and then click the Format down arrow, and click Rock.

Close your Web browser if it is open.

8   Click Find to view stations matching your search criteria.

9   On the File menu, click Exit, and then disconnect from the Internet.

Setting Up the WebTV Program Guide

important

WebTV does not support satellite TV. You must use either a cable connection or an antenna to receive over-the-airwaves broadcasts.

Microsoft WebTV for Windows brings television to your computer. And it's easy: first you install WebTV and a TV tuner card. Next, you connect your computer to a cable or an antenna. Then, you can view any TV show on your computer that you could normally view on a regular TV. In fact, you can view TV and work on your computer simultaneously.

If you own a TV, you are probably able to receive a lot of TV stations. Even in a rural area, you are likely to have access to cable or a satellite dish, both of which can offer a bewildering variety of choices. In fact, there might be so many choices that it's hard to keep track of them. Or, you might be primarily interested in a particular type of TV show—sports, comedy, or news shows, for instance—and really don't pay attention to the rest. In either case, you will find the WebTV Program Guide a useful tool for managing and organizing TV offerings in your local area. You can use the Program Guide to view all the TV shows scheduled in your area, you can search for particular types of shows or shows playing at a certain time, and you can schedule reminders to notify you when a show is about to start.

For more information, see "Watching a Television Program on Your Computer" later in this lesson.

Because the Program Guide is part of WebTV for Windows, it's also the primary means for tuning in TV shows. You can click shows to preview them, and then you can view them full screen on your monitor. To set up Program Guide, you need to download a recent listing of TV shows in your area. You can choose to have WebTV download the list, or if you have a Web connection, you can download the list from a Web site. The Web site option is usually preferable because it takes much less time.

In this exercise, you have installed a TV tuner card in your computer and hooked up cable to the tuner card. Now you are ready to set up the Program Guide to see what the TV offerings are in your area. To save time, you decide to download the TV listings from the Web.

If WebTV is installed on your computer, a WebTV icon is displayed on the Quick Launch bar; however, you might need to resize the Quick Launch bar to see the icon.

If WebTV for Windows does not show up on the Entertainment menu, you will need to install it. For help installing Windows components, see Appendix B, "Installing Microsoft Windows Me."

To complete this exercise, you will need an Internet connection, but you will not need a TV tuner card.

1   Click the Start menu, point to Programs, point to Accessories, point to Entertainment, and then click WebTV For Windows, and when prompted, connect to the Internet.

The WebTV Welcome screen appears. Voice narration accompanies the Program Guide setup.

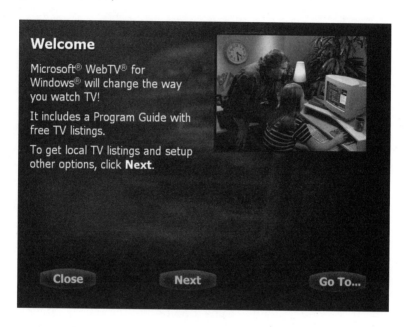

Welcome

Microsoft® WebTV® for Windows® will change the way you watch TV!

It includes a Program Guide with free TV listings.

To get local TV listings and setup other options, click **Next**.

| Close | Next | Go To... |

2   Click Next to display the Choose Viewing Options screen, and then make sure that Desktop System is selected.

3   Click Next to display the Scan For Channels screen, and then click Start Scan.

WebTV identifies the channels that you can receive with your current TV connection. This might take a few minutes.

WebTV For Windows And Data Services

tip

If you need to switch back to Windows while the Program Guide is running, press the Windows key on your keyboard. The Start menu and taskbar will be displayed. You can then open or close other programs, connect or disconnect from the Internet, and use any other Microsoft Windows Millennium Edition component. The WebTV For Windows And Data Services icon appears on the System Tray. Right-click the icon to pause WebTV.

4   Once the channels are downloaded, click Next to display the Get TV List-
     ings screen. In the Please Enter Your ZIP Code box, type your ZIP Code, and
     then click the Microsoft TV Listings link.

     WebTV connects to the Internet. A security warning is displayed, asking if
     you want to install and run the Program Guide Download Control. You will
     need this control to download the Program Guide Listings.

5   Click Yes to download the control.

     A second security warning is displayed, asking if you want to install and run
     Program Guide Loader. You will need this control to download the Program
     Guide Listings.

6   Click Yes to download the control.

     The Specify Your Location Web page appears.

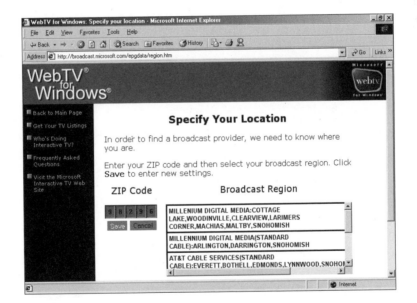

> **tip**
> WebTV downloads only a two-day schedule. You can set up Program Guide to
> download new listings daily. In the Get TV Listings Web page, scroll to the end
> of the page, and then click the Set Daily TV Listings Update link.

7   Make sure that your ZIP Code is displayed, select a broadcast region, and then click Save.

The Get TV Listings Web page appears.

8   Click Get Listings.

The programs for your area are downloaded. After a few minutes, the listings are loaded into the Program Guide.

9   Close your browser.

10   In the Get TV Listings screen, click Next.

The Assign Video Inputs screen appears.

tip

In the Assign Video Inputs screen, you can assign channels to your VCR, game player, and other devices connected to your TV so that you can control the devices from WebTV.

11   Click Next to view the Program Guide Tour.

12   Once you have finished viewing the tour, click Next, and then click Finish.

The Program Guide starts and displays the programs you have downloaded.

tip

You can rerun Program Guide setup and update Program Guide TV listings manually at any time. From the Program Guide, select the TV Configuration channel (TV C, Channel 96), and then click Watch. After a few moments the Microsoft WebTV Welcome screen appears. You can scroll through the setup screens, or you can choose an item from the Go To menu. If you want to update TV listings, click Go To, and then click Get TV Listings to download TV listings.

Using the Program Guide to View Program Listings

The Program Guide is similar to television listings in a newspaper: the listings are displayed in a grid organized by time and TV station. The TV stations are listed in a column on the left side of the grid; the TV programs are listed chronologically in rows. You can use the scroll bars to locate stations and programs. When you click a program, you will see the information about the program in the description area on the right side of the Program Guide. You might see the following icons under the title of the program.

Icon	What it means
	You have set a reminder so that you won't miss a television program that you want to watch.
	Stereo is available.
	Closed-caption is available.
	The program is a rerun.

To complete this exercise, you will need an Internet connection, but you will not need a TV tuner card.

You can also set reminders for programs that you want to watch. Once you set the reminder, a dialog box appears just before the program starts, reminding you to tune in to the program, even if you are not watching TV on your computer. In this exercise, you have downloaded TV listings for your area, and now you want to browse the local listings to see what's on. You also want to set a reminder to tune in to your local PBS station to remind you when the evening news is on.

1   Make sure that the Program Guide is running and that you have downloaded recent TV listings for your area.

5

Multimedia

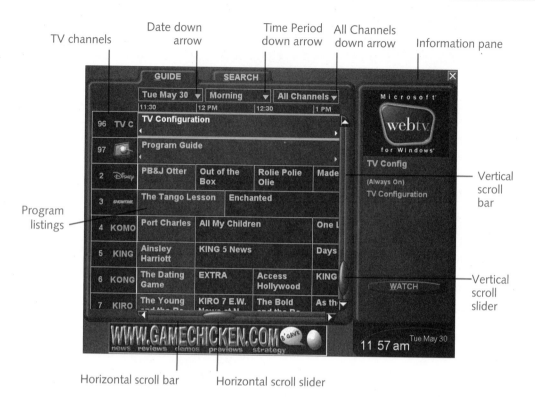

TV channels   Date down arrow   Time Period down arrow   All Channels down arrow   Information pane

Program listings

Vertical scroll bar

Vertical scroll slider

Horizontal scroll bar   Horizontal scroll slider

2   Click the Time Period down arrow, and then click Afternoon.

The Program Guide displays programs for the afternoon hours.

3   Click the Date down arrow, and then click tomorrow's date.

The Program Guide displays programs for tomorrow afternoon.

4   Drag the horizontal scroll slider to the left.

The Program Guide displays earlier programs. Each time you move the scroll slider, the Program Guide adjusts the time range displayed.

5   Click the vertical scroll bar down arrow.

The Program Guide displays additional channels. Each time you click the vertical scroll bar arrow, the Program Guide changes the channels displayed.

6   In the Program Guide window, click a program.

A blue box appears around the program timeslot, and the content information about the program appears on the right side of the WebTV window.

7   Select a PBS news show that will be aired in the future.

Because you are practicing reminders, you might want to select a show that will air within the next half hour so that you can see the reminder appear on your computer soon.

8   Click Remind.

The Remind dialog box appears.

9   Select the Once option.

You will receive a reminder five minutes before the show starts.

You also can set a reminder to alert you every time the program runs.

10   Click OK.

The Reminder icon is displayed in the Information pane.

11   Select another show. Click the Search tab, scroll down in the Categories list, and then click My Reminders.

The My Reminders list is displayed. After the program time passes, the reminder will be removed from the list.

12   Click the Guide tab.

The current program listings are displayed.

tip

Programs are often shown more than once—on the same channel or on other channels. To see a schedule of other showings, select a program, and then click Other Times.

Searching for TV Programs

If you want to search for a particular television program or for a television category such as TV news shows, you can use the Program Guide Search tab. When you search for a program, the search results include only programs that are in the current Program Guide listings.

Searching for a Particular Television Program

1   Make sure that the Program Guide is open, and then click the Search tab.

2   In the Search For box, type a term in the title of the show, the entire title of the show, or a show category like "drama."

3   Click Search.

Searching for a Television Show by Category

1   Make sure that the Program Guide Search tab is displayed.

2   In the Categories list, click a category.

5

Multimedia

Watching a Television Program on Your Computer

When you have found a program that you want to watch in the Program Guide, you simply select the show and then click Watch. The program is displayed in the Information pane. You click the program to view it full screen. When you have finished watching, you can go back to the Program Guide or exit WebTV.

In this exercise, you have found a local TV station that you are not familiar with. You want to sample one of its programs, and then you decide to add the channel to your list of favorites.

1   Make sure that the Program Guide is open and that the Guide tab is displayed.

2   Click the Time Period down arrow, and then click Now.

The Program Guide displays programs that can be currently viewed. Currently playing programs have a colored background.

3   Click a program that is playing now.

The television program is displayed in the Information pane. Note the channel number of the station that you are viewing.

4   Click Watch.

A full-screen view of the television program is displayed.

tip
You can view closed captions in WebTV. On the Program Guide toolbar, click Settings, and then select the Show Closed Captioning check box.

You can also press Alt or F10.

5   To display the Program Guide toolbar, move the pointer to the top of your screen.

Channel selector ——

6   On the Program Guide toolbar, scroll the channel selector until the number of the TV station that you are watching is displayed on the toolbar.

7   Click Add to add the channel to the toolbar.

8   Click Guide.

The toolbar closes, and the Guide tab is displayed.

9   Click the All Channels down arrow, and then click Favorites.

The channel that you added to the Program Guide toolbar is displayed.

10 Click the Favorites down arrow, and then click All Channels.

All of the current Program Guide listings are displayed.

Close

11 Click the Close button to quit WebTV.

tip

If you want to learn more about a particular TV show, you can go directly to a Web page describing that show by clicking the appropriate link in the Information pane. First, select the show that you want to learn more about, and then in the Information pane, click the show's title link. You are prompted to connect to the Internet, and your browser searches for the page referenced by the link. If your browser does not find the Web page, it will usually display links relating to the TV show. For example, if you select the PBS show Mystery! and click the Mystery! link, a number of related Mystery! links will be displayed in your browser.

Watching Interactive Television

When interactive TV is available, the Interacive TV icon has a highlighted border.

An **interactive television** show includes additional content that is broadcast along with the regular show, allowing you to interact with the show. For example, a baseball game might provide additional information about players in the game that you can view in Microsoft WebTV for Windows. Or, a talk show might include a chat room for discussing issues included in the show. The Interactive TV icon in the Program Guide indicates when a television show includes interactive content.

Interactive TV

1   In the Program Guide, find a television show that includes the Interactive TV icon.

2   Click the Interactive Television icon at the top of the screen.

3   On the Interactive TV menu, click one of the Interactive Television items.

Multimedia

5

Setting Up a Digital Camera

Digital cameras store photos electronically rather than on film. Digital cameras are becoming popular in part because photos can be immediately transferred to and viewed on your computer, and you can also edit the photos with software programs such as Kodak Imaging for Windows, which comes with Microsoft Windows Millennium Edition.

Digital cameras often come with special software for transferring photos to a computer and editing them. However, some cameras might not have this software, or their software might not be compatible with your computer or is less than user friendly. If you do not have camera software that you want to use, Windows Me has two built-in programs that you can use to transfer photos from your camera to Windows and then edit the photos.

In this exercise, you purchased a digital camera before your recent vacation and took a number of photos. You want to transfer some of the photos to your computer so that you can view and edit them.

Consult your camera's user manual to learn about the correct procedure for attaching your camera to your computer.

1   Use the cable supplied with your camera to attach the camera to your computer.

important

Depending on your hardware, the Scanner And Camera Installation Wizard may recognize your hardware and complete the installation automatically. If that happens, continue to step 8.

Steps may vary slightly depending on your camera.

2   Click the Start button, point to Settings, and then click Control Panel to display the contents of the Control Panel folder.

3   Double-click the Scanners And Cameras folder.

The Scanners And Camera folder opens.

4   Double-click the Add Device icon.

The Scanner And Camera Installation Wizard starts.

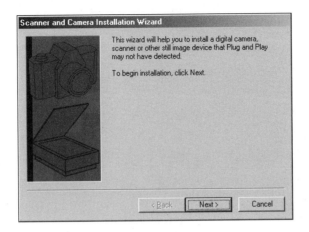

important

If your camera is not listed and you have an installation disk from the manu-
facturer, insert the disk in the CD-ROM or floppy drive, and then click Have
Disk. Follow the instructions on the screen to copy the camera software to
Windows.

5 Click Next, select your camera manufacturer and camera model, and then
click Next again.

6 Select the port your camera is plugged into, and then click Next.

*You can also
double-click
the camera
icon to start the
Windows Pic-
ture Acquisi-
tion Wizard.*

7 Type a name for the device, click Next, and then click Finish.

An icon representing your camera is displayed in the Scanners And Cameras
window. After a few seconds, the Windows Picture Acquisition Wizard starts.

8 Click Next.

The pictures stored in your camera are displayed. Selected photos are indi-
cated by a blue border.

*To select indi-
vidual pictures
to transfer to
Windows, hold
Ctrl and click
the pictures you
don't want to
transfer.*

9 Click Next, enter a name for the picture or group of pictures you selected,
and then click Finish.

The name applies to the entire group of pictures you are transferring. The
pictures are copied to a folder named after the current date.

Multimedia

5

10   Close the folder, double-click My Documents, and then double-click My Pictures.

The folder containing your pictures is located in the My Pictures folder in the My Documents folder.

11   Double-click a photo.

Image Preview opens, displaying your photo.

Using Kodak Imaging for Windows to Edit Digital Photos

Once you have transferred photos from your camera to Windows, you can edit them in Kodak Imaging for Windows, a graphics-editing program included with Microsoft Windows Millennium Edition. By default, when you double-click a graphic file, another graphics program called Image Preview starts and displays the graphic. However, you cannot edit your photos in Image Preview; you can only zoom in and out to view the photo in different sizes, rotate the photo, and print it. In Imaging, on the other hand, you can edit the photo—for example, add annotations to photos and change color types.

Annotations are text or graphics that overlay another file. In Imaging, you can make annotations separate from the photo you are editing so that they "float" over the photo. Or you can make them permanent so that they are fused to the photo and cannot be turned off. You can also change annotation properties, such as color or font sizes. To help you create the annotations, Imaging provides a number of annotation tools.

See the "Annotate a Page" topic in Imaging Help for more information about the Annotation tools.

Annotation Tool	Description
Rubber Stamp	Stamps prepared text on the photo. Imaging contains several default stamps, and you can create others.
Text From File	Attaches text from a TXT file to a photo.
Attach A Note	Attaches a note to a photo.
Text	Inserts a text box in which you can type text.
Filled Rectangle	Attaches a rectangle to the photo. Default color is black but can be changed.
Hollow Rectangle	Attaches a rectangle without a fill color.
Straight Line	Draws a straight line on a photo.
Highlighter	Highlights photo.
Freehand Line	Draws a freehand line on photo.

In Imaging, you can view graphics in almost any graphic file format, but you can only edit photos that have been saved in certain file formats:

- TIFF format. Tagged Image File Format (TIFF) is a common format for digital photos. TIFF files are larger in size than some other common file formats, such as Graphics Interchange Format (GIF) and Joint Photographic Experts Group (JPEG).
- AWD files. The format for Microsoft Fax documents. AWD files are always black and white.
- BMP files. Bitmap (BMP) files are also used in Microsoft Paint, a graphics-editing program that is included with Windows Me.

If you transfer photos from your camera to your computer using the Windows Picture Acquisition Wizard, the files will be transferred as JPG files. You will have to convert them to TIFF or BMP files to edit them in Imaging.

In this exercise, you want to prepare a photo that you took on a trip to a national park to send to your sister. You know that she plans to visit the same park, and you want to show her one of the sights that you think she should visit. You decide to add a note to the photo and then compress it before saving because you plan to e-mail it to her.

1 Click the Start button, point to Programs, point to Accessories, and then click Imaging.

Imaging for Windows starts.

2 On the File menu, click Open. Click the Look In down arrow, and then click Local Disk.

3 Double-click the Windows Me SBS folder, and then double-click Waterfall.

The Waterfall photo is displayed.

4 On the File menu, click Save As, and then in the File Name box, type **Park Photo**

You could also choose to save it as a .bmp file.

5 Make sure that TIFF Document is displayed in the Save As Type box, and then click Save.

tip
You can zoom in or out of the photo by clicking one of the Zoom buttons on the Standard toolbar, selecting a size in the Zoom list on the Standard toolbar, or choosing a command on the Zoom menu.

Attach-A-Note

6 Maximize the window, on the Annotation toolbar, right-click the Attach-A-Note button, and then click Properties.

The Attach-A-Note Properties dialog box appears.

7 Click Font, and then in the Size box, click 8.

The Attach-A-Note tool will use 8-point text.

8 Click OK twice, click the area to the right of the waterfall, and then draw a 2 inch by 2 inch square.

A note is attached to the photo.

You can resize and move the note.

9 Type **Cushman Falls. Beautiful!**

tip

You can hide or show annotations by clicking Show Annotations on the Annotation menu. You can also make annotations permanent by clicking Make Annotations Permanent on the Annotation menu. However, if you make them permanent, you will not be able to hide them.

10 Right-click the photo outside the note, and then click Properties.

The Page Properties dialog box appears.

11 Click the Compression tab, click the Compression down arrow, click LZW, and then click OK.

The file is compressed.

tip

Lempel Ziv Welch (LZW) is a compression format that does not affect the quality of the image as it is compressed. It is typically used for color photos and other color TIFF graphics files.

Copying Part of a Photo

If you are editing photos in Kodak Imaging for Windows, you might want to save only part of a photograph. For instance, if you are editing a group portrait, you can copy the image of one person from the photo and paste it into a separate file. Or, if you have a photo that contains elements that you do not want, you can select and then delete the elements.

In this exercise, you want to copy just the waterfall in the Waterfall because you would like to use it in a catalog that you are preparing at work. You also want to convert it to grayscale because the catalog will not include color photos. Then, you will print the photo so that your coworkers can review it.

Best Fit

Select Image

1 Make sure that the Park Photo is open, on the Imaging toolbar, click the Best Fit button, and then click the Select Image button.

2 Draw a box around the waterfall, including as little of the surrounding scenery as possible.

A selection box is displayed.

3 Right-click the selection box, and then click Copy.

4 On the File menu, click New, and when you are prompted to save the changes to the photo, click Yes.

The New Blank Document dialog box appears.

5 On the File Type tab, make sure that the TIFF Document option is selected, click the Color tab, click 256 Shades Of Gray, and then click OK.

A blank image document appears.

6 On the Edit menu, click Paste.

The photo is pasted into the blank document.

For more information on setting up a printer, see Lesson 7, "Backing Up Files and Adding Hardware."

7 Click outside of the photo.

The photo changes to black and white.

8 On the Zoom menu, click Actual Size.

9 On the File menu, click Print to print the photo, and then click the Close button to quit Imaging. Click No when prompted to save changes.

Close

tip

For some types of printers, such as inkjet printers, you can buy special photographic-quality paper for printing photos. Check with your printer manufacturer or a salesperson at an office supply store to learn more about the types of paper available.

Creating a Video Presentation in Movie Maker

Just as you can edit digital photos with Kodak Imaging for Windows, you can create and edit digital movies with Microsoft Movie Maker. In addition, you can work with sounds, photos, and graphics files in Movie Maker, and incorporate them into movies or slideshows. There are three steps to creating a new movie. First, you need to transfer video or other files to Movie Maker. You can import existing digital files, such as photos or films clips. You can also use Movie Maker to record existing videos. For example, you can transfer an existing videotape to Movie Maker using a VCR that is attached to your computer. As you record, the recording is converted to digital format so that you can edit it. You can also import digital photos or graphics files into Movie Maker and create a film by linking them together and adding voice narration. You can also record in Movie Maker from a Web camera or other capture devices. However, you will need a graphics card that supports video input to your computer.

Movie Maker creates clips from a longer video as it imports the files. The clips are easier to work with than an entire video.

The second step is to create the movie. To create a movie, you place segments from the movie, called *clips*, into the workspace. The workspace, which consists of a storyboard view and a timeline view, is where you edit the project. You can trim the shots to make them shorter, split shots into smaller segments, combine shots, add transitions between shots, rearrange the shots, and create voice narration. Finally, you publish your new movie so that others can view it. You can publish it on your computer and then send it to others through e-mail message or post it on a Web site.

If the Microsoft Windows Movie Maker Tour starts, click Exit.

In this exercise, you are interested in experimenting with Movie Maker. You think you might want to use it to combine and edit several family movies, but you first want to see how it works. Because you have a few video and graphics clips on your computer, you decide to make a movie from them.

important

Movie Maker requires a 300 megahertz (MHz) Pentium II or equivalent, 64 MB of RAM, and 2 GB of space on your hard disk to create movies. To record audio, you will need an audio capture device, and to record movies, you will need a video capture device.

1   Click the Start button, point to Programs, point to Accessories, and then click Windows Movie Maker.

When the clips have been created, the last clip remains selected and displays in the Monitor until the clip is no longer selected in the Collections area.

2   On the File menu, click Import, click the Look In down arrow, click Local Disk, and then double-click the Windows Me SBS folder.

3   Open the Movie folder, make sure that the Create Clips For Video Files check box is selected, and then double-click Video 1.

A message explaining that video clips are being created is displayed. After a few seconds, the clips are displayed in Movie Maker. In the Collections area, a folder named Video 1 is created.

Collections area

Monitor

Monitor Buttons area

Storyboard

Workspace area

4   On the File menu, click Import, and then double-click Video 2.

The clips are created in Movie Maker. A Video 2 folder is created beneath the Video 1 folder, and the clips are visible in the Collections area.

tip
To play a clip, click it, and then click the Play button in the Monitor Buttons area.

Play

5   On the File menu, click Import, click Graphic 1, hold down Ctrl and click Graphic 2 and Graphic 3, and then click Open.

The clips are created in the Video 2 folder.

You can also click Add To Storyboard/ Timeline on the Clip menu.

6 In the My Collections list, click the Video 1 folder. In the Collections area, click the first clip and drag it to the first frame in the storyboard, drag the second clip to the second storyboard frame, and then drag the third clip to the third storyboard frame. Click the first frame.

The frame is displayed in the Monitor.

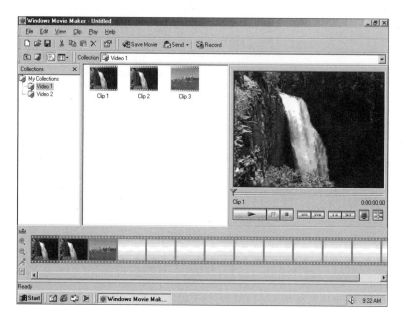

7 In the My Collections list, click the Video 2 folder. In the Collections area, click the first clip and drag it to the fourth frame in the storyboard, and then drag the second, third, and fourth clips to the following storyboard frames.

8 On the Play menu, click Play Entire Storyboard/Timeline to view your movie.

Full Screen

tip

To view the movie full screen, click the Full Screen button in the Monitor Buttons area. To return to Movie Maker, click the mouse or press Esc.

9 On the File menu, click Save Project. In the File Name box, type **My Movie Project** and then click Save.

Your project is saved in the My Videos folder in the My Documents folder.

Editing a Movie in Movie Maker

When you edit movies in Movie Maker, you can shift clips around in the storyboard. But you have more editing capabilities in the timeline. For example, you can record narration in the timeline and more easily visualize how much time each clip will take in the movie.

You have a number of options when you edit a movie. For example, you can trim clips, which means that you reduce the amount of time a clip takes by trimming off parts of it. You can split clips so that you can add material in the middle of them and combine clips to make longer clips. Also, you can create transitions between clips so that a movie flows smoothly.

In this exercise, now that you have created a movie, you want to add some graphics and narration and music for the graphics.

important

Movie Maker does not include an Undo command.

A vertical I-beam pointer appears when the clip is positioned on the storyboard.

1 Drag the Graphic 1 clip to the beginning of the storyboard.

The clip is copied to the storyboard.

2 Drag Graphic 2 to the position after the fourth clip in the storyboard.

The clip is positioned between the two original videos that make up your movie.

3 Drag Graphic 3 to the end of the storyboard clip sequence.

4 Click the Timeline button on the storyboard.

The Timeline appears, and the timeline view buttons are active. The size of the clips on the timeline are proportionate to each other—shorter clips take up less room than long clips.

Timeline

tip

The scale along the top of the timeline indicates the amount of time that the clip takes to play. For example, the first clip is about five seconds long. If you want to begin playing your movie after the first clip or graphic, click the timeline at the point you want the movie to begin playing. A play indicator appears in the timeline. Click the Play button to begin playing the movie from that point.

5   On the Timeline, select Graphic 1.

Record Narration

Make sure that your micro-phone is plugged into your computer.

6   On the Timeline, click the Record Narration button.

The Record Narration Track dialog box appears.

7   Click Record, and say **Welcome to my first movie. You will see beautiful nature scenes from the Pacific Northwest. Hope you like them, and please save your applause until the end of the movie.** into the microphone, and then click Stop.

The Save Narration Track Sound File dialog box appears.

8   In the File Name box, type **My Movie Intro** and then click Save.

The file is saved in the My Videos folder in the My Documents folder. In Movie Maker, the narration is displayed beneath the timeline and a graphic representing the narration appears in the Collection area.

Play

9   On the timeline, click Graphic 1, hold Ctrl, and then click the narration graphic. In the Monitor Buttons area, click the Play button.

The narration plays as a voice-over to the first graphic and part of the first video clip.

End Trim

If you can't see the trim points, on the View menu, click Zoom In.

10   Click Graphic 1, and position the pointer over the End Trim control in the timeline area that contains the length-of-play numbers.

An arrow appears.

11   Drag the arrow to the right until the end of Graphic 1 is at the position where the narration ends.

You have trimmed Graphic 1 so that Clip 1 will begin playing when the Graphic 1 narrative has ended.

12   On the File menu, click Import, click My Documents, double-click My Music, double-click the Beck Windows Media Audio/Video file.

The Beck audio file is imported into the Video 2 collection.

13   From the Collections area, drag the Beck file to the audio bar immediately following the narration, and then drag another copy of the Beck file to the audio bar following the first copy.

Two copies of the audio file are placed on the audio bar.

14   On the timeline, click Clip 1, and then drag it to the left until it slightly over-lays the first graphic.

You have created a transition so that the first Graphic fades out as the frames in Clip 1 fades in.

15   On the File menu, click Save Project.

16   On the timeline, click the gray area after the last graphic, and then click the Play button in the Monitor Buttons area.

Your movie plays.

tip

If you have digital photos of your family on your computer—for example, photos of your family during the last family reunion—you can use Movie Maker to make a narrated presentation of them, much like a slideshow with narration. Then, send the presentation to family and friends. They will be able to play the presentation with Media Player or other software that plays multimedia files.

17 On the Movie Maker toolbar, click Save Movie to display the Save Movie dialog box.

18 In the Title box, type **My Movie** and then click OK. In the Save As dialog box, click Save.

Once the movie has been created, a message asking if you want to watch your movie is displayed.

19 Click Yes.

Microsoft Windows Media Player starts, and your movie plays.

20 When the movie has finished playing, on the Media Player File menu, click Exit. On the Windows Movie Maker File menu, click Exit.

A message asking if you want to make a backup copy of your collections file is displayed.

21 Click No.

tip

To play a movie again, start Media Player, on the File menu, click Open, double-click the My Documents folder, double-click the My Videos folder, and then double-click the movie. To edit your movie, start Movie Maker, on the File menu, click Open, and then double-click the movie.

Lesson Wrap-Up

In Lesson 5, you learned to record voices messages, play CDs, and play multimedia files. You also listened to Web radio broadcasts, viewed local TV listings online, and watched television shows on your computer. You also downloaded photos from a digital camera and then edited the photos. Finally, you created and edited videos.

If you are continuing to the next lesson:

1   Close any open windows before continuing.

2   If you want to uninstall WebTV, in Control Panel, click the Add/Remove Programs icon, click the Windows Setup tab, and then clear the WebTV For Windows check box. Click OK twice.

3   If you want to delete the photos you downloaded from your camera, open the My Pictures folder, select the photo group you downloaded, and then click Delete.

4   If you want to delete the project and movie you created, open the My Videos folder, select the project and movie, and then click Delete.

If you are not continuing to other lessons:

1   Follow the steps in the previous section for removing items installed or used in this lesson.

2   If you are finished using your computer for now, log off Windows.

3   If you will not be using your computer for a long time, shut down Windows.

Glossary

broadband A kind of Internet transmission that includes more than one type of medium—for example, audio and video. *Broadband* can also refer to a high-speed Internet connection, such as a cable modem service.

buffering To temporarily store a file in memory until a program is ready to use it.

digital A reference to information, such as video and audio files, that is stored in a binary code, which consists of series of 1s and 0s. Digital data can be recorded on computer disks.

digital camera A camera that stores photos electronically rather than on film. Photos are stored in the camera circuitry or on a disk. The photo can then be downloaded to a computer and edited in an image-editing program.

Digital video disc (DVD) A disk similar to a CD but with a much greater capacity for storage (17 GB of content compared with 650 MB on a CD). DVDs store data digitally, and the playback of the content can far exceed the quality of data stored on videotape. DVDs require a DVD disk drive and a DVD player.

file format The structure of a file that defines how it is stored and laid out on the screen or in print. Some file formats are complex and include various types of instructions and commands used by programs, computers, printers, and other devices. Examples of complex file formats include RTF (Rich Text Format), used for documents, and TIFF (Tagged Image File Format), often used by digital cameras and image-editing programs.

interactive television A video technology in which a viewer interacts with the television programming. For example, TV sports shows might include information about players, or you might interact with contestants on TV game shows.

skins Media Player files that customize the appearance of Media Player.

streaming A technology that enables users to play multimedia files as they are being downloaded from the Internet before they have been transmitted in their entirety.

visualizations In Media Player, shapes that change with the beat of the audio that is currently playing.

Quick Reference

To record voice messages

1   Click the Start button, point to Programs, point to Accessories, point to Entertainment, and then click Sound Recorder.

2   Click the Record button, and then record a message.

3   On the File menu, click Save, locate a folder to save the file in, name the file, and then click OK.

4   To play the recording, click the Play button.

5   To copy the sound file to a document, right-click the sound file, click Copy, and then paste the file in a document.

To play music CDs

1   Click the Media Player icon on the Quick Launch bar.

2   Insert a music CD in your CD-ROM drive, and then click CD Audio.

3   To copy a track, click the Checkmark icon at the top of the first column to clear all of the track check boxes. Select a check box next to a track that you want to copy, and then click Copy Music.

4   To view the track in the Media Library, click the Pause button, and then click Media Library.

5   To create a new playlist, click New Playlist, and then in the New Playlist dialog box, type a name, and then click OK. Select the track that you copied, click Add To Playlist, and then click the name you just typed for the playlist.

6   To play the copied track, remove the CD from the CD-ROM drive, click the name of your playlist, select the track you copied, and then click the Play button.

7   Click Now Playing to view a visualization.

To play multimedia files

1   Start Media Player, and then click Media Guide.

2   Click a video link.

3   On the View menu, point to Zoom, and then click Fit To Window.

4   To view a different skin, click Skin Chooser to select a new skin, in the Skin Chooser list, click a skin type, and then click Apply Skin.

5   Click the Return To Full Mode icon that is located below the screen, and then click Now Playing.

To listen to Web radio

1   Start Media Player, and then click Radio Tuner.

2   In the Station Finder pane, Click the Find By down arrow, and then click Format. Click the Select Format down arrow, and then click a format.

3   In the Station Name list, double-click a station to listen to a broadcast.

4   To add a station to a Presets list, in the Presets pane, click the Featured down arrow, click My Presets, and then click the Add button.

5   To search for a station, in the Station Finder pane, click Search, enter the search criteria, and then click Find.

To set up the WebTV Program Guide

1   Connect to the Internet. Minimize the browser window.

2   On the Quick Launch bar, click the WebTV icon.

3   Click Next, make sure that Desktop System is selected, and then click Next.

4   Click Start Scan, Click Next, enter your ZIP Code in the Please Enter Your ZIP Code box, and then click Next again.

5   In the To Get TV Listings box, click the G-GUIDE link, click Yes, and then click Get Listings.

6   Disconnect from the Internet, and then close your browser.

7   Click Next, and then in the Choose Regular Update Time box, enter a time when you will not be using your computer.

8   Click Next three times, and then click Finish.

To use the Program Guide to view program listings

1   Make sure that Program Guide is running and that you have downloaded recent TV listings for your area.

2   To view listings for another time period, click the Time Period down arrow, and then click a selection.

3   To view listings for another date, click the Date down arrow, and then click a date.

4   To view additional listings, drag the horizontal scroll slider.

5   To view information about a program, in the Program Guide window, click a program.

6   To set a reminder, select a show that will be aired in the future, click the Remind button, and select a reminder option.

To watch a television program on your computer

1   Make sure that the Program Guide is open and that the Guide tab is displayed.

2   Click the Time Period down arrow, and then click Now.

3   Click a television program that is playing now, and then click Watch.

4   To add the channel to your favorites list, move the pointer to the top of your screen, scroll the channel selector until the number of the TV station you are watching is displayed in the toolbar, and then click the Add button.

5   To view the My Favorites list, in the Guide tab, click the All Channels down arrow, and then click Favorites.

6   To quit WebTV, click Close.

To set up a digital camera

1   Click the Start button, point to Settings, and then double-click Control Panel.

2   Double-click the Scanners And Cameras icon, and then double-click the Add Device icon.

3   Click Next, select a camera manufacturer and model, and then click Next.

4   Select the port your camera is plugged into, click Next, enter a name for the device, click Next, and then click Finish.

5 Click Next, click Next again, enter a name for the picture or group of pictures you selected, and then click Finish.

To use Kodak Imaging for Windows to edit digital photos

1 Click the Start button, point to Accessories, and then click Imaging.

2 On the File menu, click Open, and then locate and open the file you want to edit.

3 If the file is not a TIFF or BMP file, on the File menu, click Save As, type a name for the photo file, make sure that TIFF Document is displayed in the Save As Type box, and then click Save.

4 To use an annotation tool, on the Annotation toolbar, click the tool.

5 To change the properties for an annotation tool, right-click the tool.

6 To compress the photo file, right-click the photo, click Properties, click the Compression tab, click the Compression down arrow, click a compression method, and then click OK.

To copy part of a photo

1 Open the photo you want to copy from, and then on the Imaging toolbar, click Select Image.

2 On the File menu, click New.

3 On the File Type tab, make sure that TIFF Document option is selected, and then click OK.

4 On the Edit menu, click Paste.

To create a video presentation in Movie Maker

1 Click the Start button, point to Programs, point to Accessories, and then click Windows Movie Maker.

2 On the File menu, click Import, locate the file you want to import, and then double-click it.

3 In the Collections list, click an item. In the Collection area, drag the clips to the storyboard.

4 In the storyboard, click an empty frame, and then click Play on the player to view the movie you have made.

5 On the File menu, click Save Project. In the File Name box, type a name, and then click Save.

To edit a movie in Movie Maker

1   Click the Timeline button on the storyboard.

2   To add additional items to the timeline, drag them from the Collection area to the timeline.

3   To narrate an item on the timeline, select the item, and then click the Record Narration button. Click Record to record the narration, and then click Stop. In the File Name box, type a name for the narration, and then click Save.

4   To preview the narration, select the narrated item and the narration, and then in the Monitor Buttons area, click Play.

5   To trim a clip or graphic, click it, and then drag the trim point arrow to the left or right.

6   To create a transition between two clips, click the clip that is to the right, and then drag it to the left until it overlaps the first clip.

7   On the File menu, click Save Project.

8   On the timeline, click the gray area after the last graphic, and then click Play in the viewer.

9   On the Standard Movie Maker toolbar, click Save Movie to display the Save Movie dialog box. In the Title box, type a name, and then click OK. In the Save As dialog box, click Save As.

10   Once the movie has been created, in the Windows Movie Maker dialog box, click OK, and then on the File menu, click Exit.

2

Review & Practice

**ESTIMATED
TIME
20 min.**

You will review and practice how to:

✔ *Set up speed-dial numbers to dial from Microsoft Windows Millennium Edition.*

✔ *Set dialing properties to handle certain area codes and prefixes.*

✔ *Use a calling card to make long distance calls from Windows.*

✔ *Use the Address Book to keep track of contacts.*

✔ *Keep files synchronized when moving them between computers.*

✔ *Set up a game controller.*

✔ *Play CDs with Microsoft Media Player.*

✔ *Play multimedia files with Media Player.*

✔ *Play radio stations that broadcast over the Internet.*

✔ *Download local TV listings from the Web and view them.*

✔ *Use WebTV to view television programs on your computer.*

Review & Practice

In this Review & Practice, you have an opportunity to review some of the skills you developed in Lessons 4 and 5. As you are working through the review, consult the appropriate lesson if you have questions about how to complete an exercise.

Scenario

You have already helped your neighbor set up Microsoft Windows Millennium Edition on her new computer. Now, your neighbor wants to learn about some of the features that look entertaining and those that would help her with the work she brings home from her office. In particular, she has asked you to show her how to use the following Windows Me features:

For additional information on copying practice files, see the "Using the Microsoft Windows Me Step by Step CD-ROM" section at the beginning of this book.

- Microsoft Phone Dialer
- Address Book
- Dial-Up Networking
- My Briefcase
- Gaming Options
- Microsoft Windows Media Player
- Microsoft Windows WebTV

 Practice files for the lesson

To complete the exercises in the practice, you will need to use the Addresses file and the files located in the My Work folder in the Windows Me SBS folder. Before you can work with any of these exercise files, you must copy them from the Microsoft Windows Me Step by Step CD-ROM to your hard disk. You will also need a second computer and a blank disk for Step 5, a game controller for Step 6, a music CD for Step 7, and a digital camera for Step 12.

Step 1: Use Phone Dialer to Automate Phone Dialing

1   Click the Start button, point to Programs, point to Accessories, point to Communications, and then click Phone Dialer.

2   Click the first blank speed-dial button, type **Rene** type the number **111-555-1211** and then click Save.

3   Pick up your telephone receiver, and then click the speed-dial button to place the call.

4   Click Hang Up when the call is completed.

5   On the Tools menu, click Show Log to view the call log, and then click Close.

For more information about	See
Automating Phone Dialer from Windows	Lesson 4

Step 2:   Set Up a Location and an Area Code Rule in Phone Dialer

1   In Microsoft Phone Dialer, on the Tools menu, click Dialing Properties.

2   Click New, and then click OK.

3   Click Area Code Rules, and then click New. In the When Calling Within My Area Code section, type the area code **000** and then click OK.

4   In the When Calling To Other Area Codes section, click New, type the area code **111** and then click OK.

5   Close the Area Code Rules dialog box.

For more information about	See
Creating an area code rule in Phone Dialer	Lesson 4

Step 3:   Set Up a Calling Card in Phone Dialer

1   In the Dialing Properties dialog box, create a new location, and name it **Long Distance**.

2   Select the For Long Distance Calls, Use This Calling Card check box, and then click Calling Card.

3   Click New, and then name the calling card **My Card**.

4   Type the PIN number **123456**, then type the long distance access number **1-123-555-0123**, and then click Long Distance Calls.

5   In Step 1 for the calling card sequence to dial, make sure that Calling Card Phone Number is displayed; in Step 2, make sure that PIN is displayed; and in Step 3, make sure that Destination Number (Including Area Code) is displayed.

6   In the Step 1 Then Wait For box, select 10 seconds, in the Step 2 Then Wait For box, select 6 seconds, and then click OK three times.

7   In the Phone Dialer dialog box, type the long distance number that you want to call, and then click Dial.

8   Because you have entered fictitious information for this exercise, click Hang Up when the Dialing dialog box appears.

For more information about	See
Setting up Phone Dialer to use a calling card	Lesson 4

Step 4:   **Add Contacts to the Address Book**

1   Click the Start button, point to Programs, point to Accessories, and then click Address Book.

2   On the File menu, click Import, and then click Addresses.

3   Select the Address Book file "Addresses," located in the Windows Me SBS folder.

4   On the File menu, click New Group. Create a new group called **Friends**, and then click Select Members to add the people from the Addresses file to the group.

For more information about	See
Using the Address Book to keep track of contacts	Lesson 4

Step 5:   **Transfer and Update Files with Briefcase**

1   Open the My Work folder in the Windows Me SBS folder.

2   Drag the Adventure Works and Produce Letter to My Briefcase.

3   Insert a floppy disk in your floppy drive, and then drag My Briefcase to the floppy disk icon in My Computer.

4   Insert the floppy disk in a second computer's floppy drive, and then open My Briefcase.

5   Drag the files from My Briefcase to the desktop.

6   Open the Adventure Works file, change **Seattle** to **Olympia**, and then save and close the letter. Open the Produce Letter file, and change **Brothers** to **Company**, and then save and close the letter.

7   Update the letters in Briefcase, transfer the floppy disk to the first computer, and then update the files on the first computer. Remove the floppy disk from the computer.

For more information about	See
Keeping transferred files synchronized using Briefcase	Lesson 4
Updating My Briefcase files	Lesson 4

Step 6:   **Calibrate a Game Controller**

1   In Control Panel, open Gaming Options.

2   Click Add, select the controller, and then click OK.

3   Click Properties, and then in the Settings tab, click Calibrate. Make sure that the controller is functioning properly.

4   Click Finish, click OK twice, and then close Control Panel.

For more information about	See
Adding and calibrating a game controller	Lesson 4

Step 7:   Play a Music CD

1   Click the Start button, point to Programs, point to Accessories, point to Entertainment, and then click Windows Media Player.

2   Insert a music CD in your CD-ROM drive, and then click Audio CD.

3   Select the tracks that you want to copy, click Copy Music, click the Pause button, and then click Media Library.

4   Click the plus sign (+) next to Audio, and then click the plus sign next to Album.

5   Click New Playlist, and then in the New Playlist dialog box, type **CD Tracks** and then click OK.

6   Click the plus sign next to My Playlists, select the track that you copied, click Add To Playlist, and then click Add To CD Tracks.

7   Remove the CD from the CD-ROM drive, and then click CD Tracks. Click the Play button, and then click the Stop button.

For more information about	See
Playing music CDs	Lesson 5

Step 8:   Play Multimedia Files

1   In Media Player, click Media Guide, and then connect to the Internet.

2   Click a video link that is compatible with your connection speed.

3   When you are finished viewing the clip, on the File menu, click Close.

For more information about	See
Using Media Player to play multimedia files	Lesson 5

Step 9:   Listen to a Radio Station over the Internet

1   In Media Player, click Radio Tuner.

2   In the Station Finder pane, click the Find By down arrow, and then click Format. In the Select Format box, click the down arrow, and then click Classical.

3   In the Station Name list, double-click a station to listen to a broadcast.

4   To add the station to a new playlist, in the Presets pane, click the Featured down arrow, and then click Create Preset List.

5   Type **My List** click Add, and then click OK.

6   In the Presets pane, click the Featured down arrow, and then click My List.

7   Click Add.

For more information about	See
Listening to Web radio	Lesson 5

Step 10:   Download TV Listings to WebTV

1   Click the Start button, point to Programs, point to Accessories, point to Entertainment, and then click WebTV For Windows.

2   In the WebTV Welcome screen, click Next twice, and then click Start Scan for channels that you can receive with your TV connection.

3   Click Next, type your ZIP Code, click Next, and then click Go To The Microsoft TV Listings Web Site to download the listings.

4   Click Get Listings.

5   Disconnect from the Internet, and then quit your browser.

6   In WebTV, enter regular update information, and then complete the WebTV setup.

For more information about	See
Setting up the WebTV program guide	Lesson 5

Step 11:   Use WebTV to Watch a TV Program

1   In the Program Guide, click the Time Period down arrow, and then click Now.

2   Click a program that is playing now, and then click Watch.

3   When you have finished viewing the program, close the Program Guide.

For more information about	See
Using the Program Guide to view program listings	Lesson 5

Step 12: Install a Camera

1   Make sure that your camera is attached to your computer. Click the Start button, point to settings, and then double-click Control Panel.

2   Double-click the Scanners And Cameras folder, and then double-click the Add Device icon.

3   Work through the steps in the Scanner And Camera Installation Wizard.

4   Work through the steps in the Windows Picture Acquisition Wizard.

5   Close the folder, double-click My Documents, and then double-click My Pictures.

6   Open the My Pictures folder, and then double-click a photo.

For more information about	See
Setting up a digital camera	Lesson 5

If you are continuing to the next lesson

1   Close all open folders.

2   To delete the speed-dial number from the "Use Phone Dialer to Automate Phone Dialing" practice, open Phone Dialer. On the Edit menu, click Speed Dial. In the Edit Speed Dial dialog box, click the number button, select the name, and press Delete. Then, select the number to dial, press Delete, and then click Save.

3   To delete the new location area code rule from the "Set Up a Location and an Area Code Rule in Phone Dialer" practice, on the Tools menu, click Dialing Properties, make sure that My Location(2) is selected, click Remove, and then click Yes.

4   To delete the Calling Card information from the "Set Up a Calling Card in Phone Dialer" practice, in the Dialing Properties dialog box, click Calling Card, select Long Distance, and then click Remove.

5   To delete the addresses that you imported in the "Add Contacts to the Address Book" practice, start the Address Book, select the names Anas Abbar, Eva Corets, and Sean P. Alexander. To delete the group, right-click the group, and then click Delete.

6   To delete the camera you installed in the "Install a Camera" practice, open the Scanners And Cameras folder, right-click the icon of the camera you installed, and then click Delete.

If you are not continuing to other lessons

1   Undo the changes you made during the Review & Practice by following steps 2 through 6 in the previous section.

2   If you are finished using your computer for now, log off Windows.

3   If you will not be using your computer for a long time, shut down Windows.

PART 3

Tuning Up Microsoft Windows Me

LESSON

6

Maintaining Windows and Windows Files

**ESTIMATED
TIME
30 min.**

After completing this lesson, you will be able to:

✔ *Update your Microsoft Windows Millennium Edition installation from the Microsoft Windows Update Web site.*

✔ *Restore Windows to a previous state when you have trouble making changes to your system.*

✔ *Delete unneeded files from your hard disk.*

✔ *Prevent hard disk problems by running maintenance utilities.*

✔ *Set up maintenance utilities and other programs so that they run automatically according to a schedule that you create.*

✔ *Create power settings that save energy when your computer is idle.*

Keeping Microsoft Windows Millennium Edition running in top form requires little effort. As with any program, however, Windows Me can at times benefit from some maintenance so that it keeps running the way you want it to. For example, Microsoft provides free routine updates to Windows Me that you can download from the Internet to enhance or extend the operating system. In addition, Windows Me itself comes with several utilities that you can use to keep it running smoothly. Windows Me also provides several ways to automate these tasks so that updating and maintenance is done in the background.

In this lesson, you will learn how to update Windows Me so that your version has the latest enhancements. You will learn how to restore Windows to a previous, stable state in case something goes wrong with a program installation. You will also learn how to perform hard disk maintenance, such as deleting unneeded files and checking your hard disk for problems. You will then learn how to set up a schedule so that these and other tasks can run automatically, based on a schedule that you create. Finally, you will learn about Windows Me power settings that will help you save energy when your computer is idle.

Practice files for the lesson ➡ No practice files are required to complete the exercises in this lesson.

Keeping Windows Up to Date

An advantage of using the Microsoft Windows Millennium Edition operating system is that even though you have the final product installed on your computer, you can still add enhancements to it, free of charge, from Microsoft. In fact, Microsoft continues to update Windows Me so that you have the latest in fixes, updates, and enhancements. To get the updates easily, Windows Me includes the Windows Update feature, which you can use to download many kinds of updates from the Microsoft Windows Update Web site—for instance, new screen savers, components that support other languages, problem fixes, and program previews. The number and kind of offerings depend on what is currently available from Microsoft. Some of the common offerings are listed below.

Update	For
Critical Updates	Fixing known, serious problems with Windows Me, such as security issues that can affect your computer. Microsoft advises that you always download Critical Updates.
Picks of the Month	Featured program updates, such as a new version of MSN Instant Messenger Service or other programs that are part of Windows Me.
Recommended Updates	Enhancing Windows Me components, such as updates to Windows Help. Recommended Updates are not critical but usually make Windows Me run better or safer, and can otherwise enhance or extend Windows components.
Additional Windows Features	New or updated programs or features. Some of the offerings are created by Microsoft, and others might be offered by other software vendors. For example, Microsoft has offered an update to its virtual reality Web viewer, the VRML Viewer.
Device Drivers	Updates to software necessary to run hardware used by your computer, such as printers and modems.

For information on setting up an Internet connection, see Lesson 2, "Setting Up Internet Accounts and E-mail."

To update Windows Me, you first connect to the Windows Update Web site. When you connect, the site scans your system to see what you have already installed so that it can recommend updates specific to your installation of Windows Me. During this process, to ensure your privacy, no information is sent to Microsoft. When the list of recommended updates is displayed, you can choose as few or as many of the updates as you like. The Windows Update site also indicates which updates are new or updated for the month and which are fun or best for advanced users. In addition, approximate download times are provided.

In this exercise, you want to check the Windows Update Web site to see if there are components that you want to download. You connect to the site, review the list of updates, and then choose one to download.

1   Click the Start button, click Windows Update, and when prompted, connect to the Internet.

The Microsoft Windows Update site appears.

important

The first time that you open the Product Updates page, a message prompting you to install and run Microsoft Active Setup is displayed. This program is necessary for downloading updates from the site. You must click OK to use the Windows Update feature.

important

If Microsoft has updated the Windows Me system files, you will be prompted to download the new system files when you connect to the Windows Update site. You must install the new system files before you can continue with updating other Windows components.

2   Click the Product Updates link.

A message explaining that the products list is being updated is displayed, and then the Product Updates Select Software page appears.

There are no updates displayed in this screen sample.

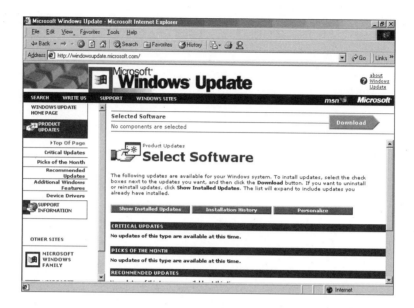

3   Select the component that you want to download.

A message near the top of the page indicating the file size and download time is displayed.

If you are unsure how to install or download updates, print the download instructions before you continue.

4   Click the Read This First link located after the description of the update you have selected.

A message describing how to download the component and how to use the component once it is downloaded is displayed. Other information might be included that describes the update.

5   Click the Back To Product Updates link to return to the Product Updates page.

tip

You can click the Show Installed Updates, Installation History, and Personalize buttons to view more information about updates or to customize the Product Updates page.

6   Click Download.

The Download Checklist page appears. You can confirm your download selections, and view and print download instructions.

You might need to manually install the update before you can use it. See the update instructions for details.

7   Click Start Download, read the license agreement, and then click Yes to continue with the download.

The update is downloaded to your computer, and then a page appears to indicate that the download and installation was successful.

If you want to download additional updates, click Back.

8   Quit your browser, and then disconnect from the Internet.

tip

If you have downloaded and installed a Windows update and want to uninstall it, click the Start button, point to Programs, point to Accessories, point to System Tools, and then click System Information. Click Tools, and then click Update Wizard Uninstall.

Updating Windows Automatically

When you update Microsoft Windows Millennium Edition manually, you need to remember to log on to the Microsoft Windows Update Web site, check the site for updates, and then download updates relevant to you. However, you can set Windows Me to automatically download and install critical updates. To set up Windows for automatic updates, go to Control Panel, and then click Automatic Updates to open the Automatic Updates dialog box in which you have several options:

- You can set Windows to automatically download updates when you are connected to the Internet. The updates are downloaded in the background when you are connected to the Internet so that the update process does not interfere with your work. Once the updates are downloaded, you can install them. If you choose not to install an update, Windows deletes it from your computer.

tip

A message appears periodically while you are connected to the Internet to let you know that you can set up Automatic Updates. If you click Yes, the Automatic Wizard starts, and you can use it to set up Automatic Updates.

(continued)

continued

■ You can have Windows notify you before downloading updates. An update icon in the taskbar signals that the updates are ready to be downloaded. You can also choose not to download them at that time.

■ You can turn off Automatic Updates and check the Windows Update Web site at your convenience.

If you decide not to install updates, the files are not deleted but marked as hidden files. You can install the updates later by locating the hidden updates and then installing them. To install the updates, click Restore Hidden Items in the Update Settings dialog box.

Restoring Windows

Occasionally, you might install new software that causes problems with Microsoft Windows Millennium Edition or with other software. For example, you might install a new e-mail program that interferes with connecting to the Internet. Or, you might install a scanner whose driver software interferes with the operation of your printer. Windows Me prevents serious damage to your system files with System File Protection (SFP), a feature that checks important system files to make sure that they are not damaged or erased when you install other software. SFP operates in the background as you use your computer; you don't need to turn it on or change any settings.

Even with SFP working in the background, you still might run into other problems with Windows Me, such as damaged or erased files caused by an errant program. You can try uninstalling the software, but sometimes even that will not help.

When uninstalling the software doesn't solve the problem, you can use System Restore, which will undo changes you or the software made to Windows Me. As you use Windows Me, System Restore records any changes you make to Windows Me and other software on your computer. For example, System Restore creates checkpoints every 10 hours of operation. These checkpoints are snapshots of how your computer is set up at that point. System Restore also can also keep track of events, such as the installation of a new program, and create a snapshot of your system before the event occurred. If Windows is not operating correctly and you aren't sure what is causing the problem, you can restore Windows to a time when you know Windows was operating correctly—the previous day, for instance, or a week before. You can also create restore points, which are specific instances that you can restore Windows to. For example, if you think that installing a game might interfere with how Windows operates, you can create a restore point immediately before installing the game. If the game does create problems, you can restore Windows to the point before you installed the game. When you restore Windows Me, all current system and software files are replaced by the files that were working before changes were made. If you restore to the wrong date or wrong restore point, you can undo the Windows restore operation.

To use System Restore, you need at least 200 MB of hard disk space or space on the disk partition where Windows Me is installed. Some programs might require additional space to store backup information. If your hard disk or disk partition does not have 200 MB of free space, System Restore is disabled when Windows Me is installed. You would then have to free up additional space to enable it.

important

To protect your document files, System Restore does not write over documents that have common file name extensions, such as .doc for Microsoft Word documents or .vsd for Visio drawings. In addition, System Restore also does not replace any documents in the My Documents folder. To assure that your documents are protected from being changed by System Restore, make sure that they are created with a program recognized by System Restore, or store them in My Documents.

tip

If System Restore was not enabled when you installed Windows Me, you can enable it. In Control Panel, double-click System, click the Performance tab, and then click File System. Click the Troubleshooting tab, and then clear the Disable System Restore check box.

You can reverse any change that System Restore makes to your computer.

In this exercise, you have installed a new program that seems to have affected how your system works. You decide to use System Restore to restore you system to its previous state.

1   Quit any open programs. Click the Start button, point to Programs, point to Accessories, point to System Tools, and then click System Restore.

      The System Restore Wizard starts.

*For a demon-
stration of how
to restore
Windows, in
the Multimedia
folder on the
Microsoft
Windows Me
Step by Step
CD-ROM,
double-click
RestoreWindows.*

tip

To create a specific restore point, click Create A Restore Point, click Next, and then type a name for the restore point. A good time to create a restore point is just before making any changes to your system.

2   Click Restore My Computer To An Earlier Time, and then click Next.

A calendar is displayed, with a list of system checkpoints for the current day, which is selected. If you have set up restore points, they will be listed as well.

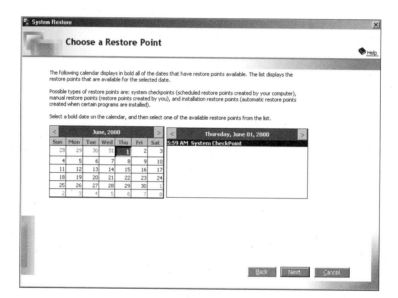

3   In the calendar, click a date you want to restore to. In the list of restore points, choose a time, and then click Next.

A message reminding you to close all open files and programs is displayed. The restore point you have selected is listed in the wizard screen.

4   Click OK, and then click Next.

The Restoration In Progress screen appears, and the restore process starts. After several minutes, your system is restored, and then your computer restarts. A message indicating that your system has been restored successfully is displayed.

5   Click OK.

> **tip**
> To undo the restore, start System Restore again, and then click Undo My Last Restoration. You can also restore to another date. In the second wizard screen, select the alternative day and time you want to restore to.

Cleaning Up Your Hard Disk

Disk Cleanup can also be used on floppy disks and other removable disks attached to your system, such as Iomega Zip disks.

The more you use Microsoft Windows Millennium Edition, the more likely it is that you will accumulate files that you do not need. For example, some programs might store **temporary files** in the Windows Temp folder, which are not deleted when the program closes. Or, your Recycle Bin can become the repository of all the files you meant to get rid of if you forget to occasionally empty it. After some period of time, you can end up with a lot of disk space taken up by unwanted files. You can use the Disk Cleanup utility to quickly delete unneeded files and, as a result, improve the performance of your computer. Of course, you can locate and delete unwanted files by searching through your hard disk. Disk Cleanup makes the process easier by providing a central location from which you can perform your cleanup chores.

In the Disk Cleanup dialog box, you can click the following tabs to set up how you want Disk Cleanup to function:

- Disk Cleanup tab. You can select the kinds of files you want to delete—temporary Internet files, offline Web pages, files in the Recycle Bin, and temporary program files. When you choose a file type to delete, an explanation of the file type is displayed in the Description box.

- More Options tab. You can choose to delete Windows components or other installed programs that you do not use or limit the amount of space System Restore can use.

In this exercise, you want to delete any unneeded files that are taking up disk space on your computer, so you decide to run Disk Cleanup.

1   Click the Start button, point to Programs, point to Accessories, point to System Tools, and then click Disk Cleanup.

   The Select Drive dialog box appears.

2   Make sure that your hard disk drive is displayed in the Drives box, and then click OK.

tip

To view an explanation of each file group, select a check box in the Files To Delete list, and then view the explanation in the Description area. You can also view the actual files in each group by clicking the button below the Description box. Note that the button name changes depending on the group selected in the Files To Delete list.

The Disk Cleanup dialog box appears. The Temporary Internet Files check box and Downloaded Program Files check box are selected by default, and the amount of space that can be reclaimed for each file type is listed.

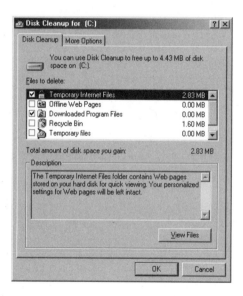

3   In the Files To Delete list, select the Recycle Bin check box and Temporary Files check box, and then click OK.

A message asking if you want to permanently delete the selected files is displayed.

4   Click Yes to delete the files.

Fixing Hard Disk Problems
Before They Happen

ScanDisk can also be used on floppy disks and other removable disks attached to your system, such as Zip disks.

As you use Microsoft Windows Millennium Edition, you might encounter programs that don't run correctly or other glitches that can affect how well your hard disk operates. For example, Windows Me can misplace files or cause problems in a file or folder if an application shuts down unexpectedly. To avoid problems like these, Windows Me includes ScanDisk, a utility that finds and fixes errors in files and folders on your hard disk. With ScanDisk, you can fix small problems before they become bigger problems.

You can run ScanDisk at any time. In fact, if your computer shuts down unexpectedly, such as when a program crashes, ScanDisk runs automatically when you restart your computer. When you start ScanDisk, you can have it run a Standard test, which checks for problems in files or folders, or you can have it run a Thorough test, which checks for problems in files and folders but also checks the physical surface of your disk for problems. The Standard test is much faster and is the default setting for ScanDisk. ScanDisk checks for the following three types of errors:

- Cross-linked files. Cross-linked files are two or more files that share the same portion of your hard disk. If files are cross-linked, the program you created them in might not be able to read them, or your computer might shut down unexpectedly when trying to access them.

- Lost **file fragments**. Lost file fragments are separate fragments of a larger file that are stored randomly on a hard disk. Lost file fragments often occur on hard disks that have little free space and can make reading and writing to the hard disk slower.

- Invalid file information. Invalid file information includes incorrect information about file names and the date and time when files were created or modified. ScanDisk can also find the duplicates of broken files, if any exist on your hard disk. If your files have any of these errors, you might not be able to find or use them.

The ScanDisk default settings determine how it fixes these errors. In most cases, the default settings are best, and you should not need to change them. ScanDisk is also set up to display a summary of any problems it finds and to create a log file, which is located in the root directory of your hard disk and is named Scandisk.log.

In this exercise, you notice that your hard disk has seemed to slow down unexpectedly. You decide to run ScanDisk to head off any hard disk problems you might have.

Before running
ScanDisk, close
any programs
that are run-
ning.

1   Click the Start button, point to Programs, point to Accessories, point to System Tools, and then click ScanDisk.

The ScanDisk dialog box appears.

Help

tip

To change the ScanDisk defaults, click Advanced. To learn about the advanced options, in the ScanDisk Advanced Options dialog box, click the Help button in the dialog box title bar, and then click an option.

2   Select the Automatically Fix Errors check box.

Any errors ScanDisk encounters will be fixed automatically. If the check box is not selected, you will be prompted each time ScanDisk encounters errors so that you can specify how the errors will be fixed.

3   Click Start.

ScanDisk checks your hard disk and indicates progress on the progress indicator. After a few minutes, the ScanDisk results are displayed.

4   Click Close to close the ScanDisk results, and then in the ScanDisk dialog box, click Close.

Keeping Your Hard Disk Running Smoothly

Another hard disk utility is Disk Defragmenter, which **defragments,** or reorganizes, your hard disk so that files are located in a single area, rather than stored in small pieces in different areas.

Whereas ScanDisk fixes lost file fragments, Disk Defragmenter makes the storage of files more efficient by placing file information in the same area, or **cluster,** on your hard disk. As Windows Me writes file information to your hard disk, it might have to place part of the information in one place and the rest of the information in another if there is not a cluster large enough to accommodate all of it. If that happens, accessing the files can take more time because your hard disk has to search for all the pieces of the files that are scattered in different locations. Disk Defragmenter puts all of the disconnected pieces in a single location, thus speeding up the hard disk operation. As with ScanDisk, the Disk Defragmenter default settings should not have to be changed.

Depending on the size and state of your hard disk, Disk Defragmenter can take over 20 minutes to finish.

In this exercise, you run Disk Deframenter to complete the maintenance on your hard disk.

> **tip**
> To change the Disk Defragmenter settings, in the Select Drive Dialog box, click Settings. To learn about the advanced options, in the Disk Defragmenter Settings dialog box, click the Help button in the dialog box title bar, and then click a setting.

[?]

Help

In the Select Drive dialog box, you can click Settings to view or change the Disk Defragmenter settings.

1   Click the Start button, point to Programs, point to Accessories, point to System Tools, and then click Disk Defragmenter.

   The Select Drive dialog box appears with Drive C selected.

2   Click OK to start Disk Defragmenter.

3   Click Show Details, and then in the Defragmenting Drive dialog box, click Legend.

   A graphic display of your hard disk appears, and a legend opens that provides a key for interpreting the symbols used in the display.

Maintaining Windows/Files
6

The Defrag Legend window doesn't have to be open while you defrag your hard disk.

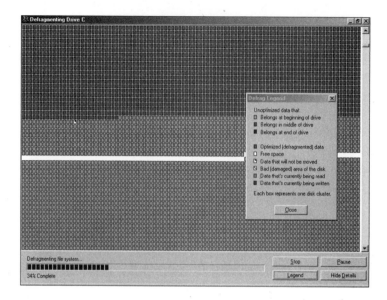

4   When your hard disk has been defragmented, a message asking if you want to quit Disk Defragmenter is displayed. Click Yes.
Disk Defragmenter quits.

Automating Windows Maintenance

You need to know how to manually start and use Windows Maintenance tools like Disk Cleanup, ScanDisk, and Disk Defragmenter for times when a program unexpectedly quits and you suspect it might have affected your hard disk, for example. However, the tasks that the utilities accomplish should also be a routine part of using your computer. By running them at predetermined intervals, you can help keep your computer in top shape and avoid problems.

You use the Microsoft Windows Millennium Edition Maintenance Wizard to automate these maintenance tasks. In the Maintenance Wizard, you can choose which of the utilities you want to run automatically, adjust their settings, and then set up a schedule. You can set up a convenient day and time slot when you won't need your computer during which you want the utilities to run. For example, if you don't use your computer in the early morning hours, you can set the schedule from midnight to 3:00 A.M. so that the utilities run without interfering with your work. Of course, your computer must be running during that time period.

The Maintenance Wizard also has an Express setting in which you can identify the time slot, and all the other settings are made for you.

Setting Up the Maintenance Wizard

1   Click the Start button, point to Programs, point to Accessories, point to System Tools, and then click Maintenance Wizard.

2   When you are asked what you want to do, click the Change My Maintenance Settings Or Schedule, and then click OK. You have to run the wizard once before you can change your settings or schedule.

3   In the first wizard screen, click the Express option to use the default settings. To set up a custom maintenance schedule and change the default settings for each utility, click the Custom option.

4   Click Next to change or review the settings.

5   Click Finish when you are done.

Turning Off the Maintenance Wizard

By default, the Maintenance Wizard is set up to run Disk Cleanup, ScanDisk, and Disk Defragmenter using the Express maintenance setting. If you do not want the maintenance tools to run automatically, follow these steps:

1   Click the Start button, point to Programs, point to Accessories, point to System Tools, and then click Maintenance Wizard.

2   When prompted, click the Change My Maintenance Settings Or Schedule, and then click OK.

3   In the first Maintenance Wizard screen, click Custom, and then click Next, and then click Next again.

4   In the Speed Up Programs screen, click No in the options that you don't want to run automatically, click Next three times, and then click Finish.

Scheduling Tasks

For more information on using Windows user profiles, see Lesson 1, "Customizing Windows for Personal Use."

Microsoft Windows Millennium Edition provides yet another tool for automating tasks—the Task Scheduler. You can use the Task Scheduler to schedule Windows Updates and maintenance, but it is especially useful for scheduling other tasks, such as starting programs that you frequently use. In fact, you can use the Task Scheduler to schedule and run just about any program you have installed in Windows. For example, you might set the Task Scheduler to launch your word-processing program every time you start Windows or log on to Windows using your Windows profile.

Maintaining Windows/Files

6

Task Scheduler is set up to run in the background each time you start Windows. You can schedule a task to run daily, weekly, monthly, or at certain other times, such as when you start your computer or when it is idle. The Scheduled Tasks folder lists all of the tasks currently scheduled. From the Scheduled Tasks folder, you can add and remove tasks, edit task schedules, pause the Scheduler or a specific task, turn off the Task Scheduler, and view the task log. You can also change task settings from the Task Scheduler folder.

In this exercise, you always check your e-mail when you first start your computer, so you decide to set up Task Scheduler to start Microsoft Outlook Express whenever you start Windows Me.

> **tip**
> Several applications are included in Task Scheduler by default. All of them are part of the Windows Me set of tools that help safeguard your computer from software problems.

1   Click the Start button, point to Programs, point to Accessories, point to System Tools, and then click Scheduled Tasks.

The Scheduled Tasks folder opens.

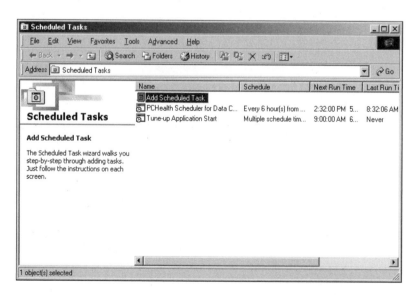

2   Double-click the Add Scheduled Task icon.

The Scheduled Task Wizard starts.

To locate a program not listed in the Scheduled Task Wizard list of applications, click Browse.

3 Click Next, scroll down in the Application list, click Outlook Express, and then click Next.

4 In the next wizard screen, click When I Log On, click Next, and then click Finish.

After a few seconds, Outlook Express is displayed in the Scheduled Tasks folder list.

important

If you have not set up Windows profiles, you will need to restart Windows to run Outlook Express automatically with Task Scheduler.

5 Close the Scheduled Tasks folder, click the Start button, click Log Off, and then click Yes.

The Enter Password dialog box appears.

tip

If you want to stop a task in progress, open the Scheduled Tasks folder, right-click the task, and then click End Task.

6 Type or click your user name, type your password, and then click OK.

After a few minutes, Windows starts, Outlook Express starts, and then the Connect To dialog box appears.

7 If necessary, type your password, and then click Connect.

After a few seconds, you are connected to your Internet service provider (ISP), and Outlook Express downloads your e-mail messages.

8 When you are finished downloading and replying to your e-mail messages, quit Outlook Express, and then disconnect from your Internet connection.

tip

Task Scheduler keeps a log of the most recently run tasks. To view the log, open Task Scheduler, and on the Advanced menu, click View Log. The most recently run tasks are listed in the top half of the log.

Changing Task Scheduler Settings

Once you have Task Scheduler set up, you might want to change some of the Task Scheduler settings or even turn it off.

Changing Settings

1   In the Scheduled Tasks folder, right-click the task, and then click Properties.

2   Click the Schedule or Settings tab, and then make the changes.

3   To learn about items in the Properties dialog box, click the Help button on the title bar, and then click the item you want to learn about.

Help

If you turn off Task Scheduler, Windows Update and the tasks scheduled with the Main-tenance Wizard will still run automatically.

Deleting Tasks or Turning Off Task Scheduler

1   To remove individual tasks from Task Scheduler, in Task Scheduler, right-click the task, and then click Delete.

2   To turn off Task Scheduler, in the Scheduled Tasks folder, click the Advanced menu, and then click Stop Using Task Scheduler.

Turning On Task Scheduler

1   Click the Start button, point to Programs, point to Accessories, point to System Tools, and then click Scheduled Tasks.

2   On the Advanced menu, click Start Using Task Scheduler.

Managing Power Settings

Microsoft Windows Millennium Edition includes a program you can use to reduce the amount of energy used by your computer. For example, if you don't use your keyboard or mouse for a period of time, you can choose to have your computer go into standby mode. When your computer goes into standby mode, the monitor screen turns off and your hard disk stops spinning. When you press a key on the keyboard or move the mouse, the computer immediately returns to the same screen as before it went to standby. The kinds of power settings available to you will depend on your computer manufacturer and the kind of computer you have. For example, laptop computers often have power settings that alert you when you have a low battery. Windows Me provides three power settings:

■ Automatic Hard Disk And Monitor Shut Down: Your monitor and hard disks turn off after a period of time that you specify. To start your computer again, you can move the mouse or press a key on the keyboard. Use this power setting when you will be away from your computer for short periods of time.

■ Standby: Your computer is idle but remains available for immediate use. Any data in your computer memory will be lost when your computer goes on standby if your power accidentally goes off. For example, if you make changes to a document but do not save them, the changes will be lost when your computer is on standby, and your power is interrupted. To start your computer again, you can move the mouse or press a key on the keyboard. Use this power setting when you will be away from your computer for longer periods of time.

■ Hibernation: Your computer is turned off after any open files are saved. When you restart, any program that was open is restored to the state it was in before your computer went into hibernation. For example, if Microsoft Word were open and you had not saved the document you were working on, Windows Me would first save the document before going into hibernation, and then when you restarted your computer, Word would be restored to its open state. To exit hibernation, you press the power button on your computer. Use this setting when you will be away from your computer for extended periods of time, such as overnight.

tip

If Hibernate does not show up in the Power Schemes dialog box and you know that your computer supports it, you might need to enable it. To do so, in the Power Options Properties dialog box, click the Hibernate tab, and then select the Enable Hibernate Support check box.

You can set up power schemes in Windows Me, which are combinations of one or more power settings. Windows Me includes the Home/Office Desk, Portable/ Laptop, and Always On power schemes. The Home/Office Desk power scheme turns off the monitor after 15 minutes and turns the hard disk off after 30 minutes. The Portable/Laptop power scheme turns off the monitor after 15 minutes, turns off the hard disk after 30 minutes, turns on standby after 20 minutes, and turns on hibernation after one hour. You can also set up custom power schemes to suit your own schedule.

Maintaining Windows/Files

6

important

The specific power settings available on your computer might vary, depending on the type and manufacturer of the computer you have. The Power Options Properties dialog box displays only the options that are available for your computer. For more information on the power settings supported by your computer, consult your computer documentation or computer manufacturer.

In this exercise, you want to set up a power scheme for your computer, but first you want to experiment with the power schemes to see how they work. You decide to test standby first.

1   Click the Start button, point to Settings, and then click Control Panel.

2   Double-click Power Options to open the Power Options Properties dialog box.

To view the default power schemes, click the Power Schemes down arrow, and then click the scheme whose settings you want to view. Click Apply to enable that scheme.

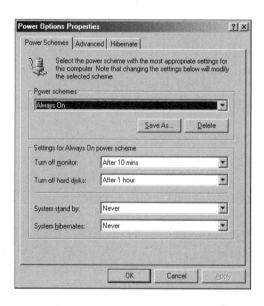

tip

To set advanced power options, click the Advanced tab. You can show the Power Schemes icon on the system tray, and you can have Windows Me prompt for a password before it goes off standby or hibernate.

3   Click the System Standby down arrow, and then click After 3 Mins.

4   Click Save As, type **Test** and then click OK.

The power scheme is named Test.

5   Click Apply.

After your computer is idle for three minutes, standby will start.

6   Move the mouse or press a key to return your system to the previous active state.

7   In the Power Options Properties dialog box, click Delete, and then click Yes to delete the Test power scheme.

tip

To quickly put your computer into standby or hibernation, click the Start button, click Shut Down, click the What Do You Want The Computer To Do down arrow, and then click Stand By or Hibernate.

Lesson Wrap-Up

In Lesson 6, you learned to update Microsoft Windows Millennium Edition by connecting to the Microsoft Windows Update Web site, and then you learned how to restore Windows Me to a previous state. You also learned how to use Windows utilities to clean up your hard disk and fix hard disk problems, and to set up the utilities and other programs to run according to a schedule that you created. Finally, you learned how to set up a customized power setting to save energy while your computer is idle.

If you are continuing to the next lesson:

1   Close any open windows before continuing.

2   To delete the Microsoft Outlook Express task that you scheduled in this lesson, double-click the Task Scheduler icon on the System Tray, right-click the task, and then click Delete.

If you are not continuing to other lessons:

1   Follow the steps in the previous section for removing items installed or used in this lesson.

2   If you are finished using your computer for now, log off Windows.

3   If you will not be using your computer for a long time, shut down Windows.

Glossary

cluster A group of storage areas on a hard disk that Windows uses to read and write information.

defragment To rewrite parts of a file to adjacent areas on a hard disk to increase the speed of access and retrieval. See *file fragment*.

file fragment A part of a file that is broken off as it is stored on a hard disk. Fragmentation occurs frequently when files are added to and then saved on a hard disk that is almost full, which can eventually slow down reading and writing to the disk. See *defragment*.

temporary file A file created on a hard disk or in memory to be used temporarily by a program and then discarded.

Quick Reference

To keep Windows up to date

1   Click the Start button, click Windows Update, and when prompted, connect to the Internet.

2   Click the Product Updates link, and then select a component to download.

3   Click the Read This First link located after the description of the update you have selected.

4   Click the Back To Product Updates link to return to the update page.

5   Click Download, click Start Download, read the license agreement, and then click Yes to continue with the download.

To restore Windows

1   Make sure that all open programs are closed. Click the Start button, point to Programs, point to Accessories, point to System Tools, and then click System Restore.

2   Click Next, and in the Click A Day calendar, select the day to which you want to restore your system. In the Click A Point During That Day list, select the time during that day to which you want to restore your system.

3   Click OK, and then click Next.

To clean up your hard disk

1   Click the Start button, point to Programs, point to Accessories, point to System Tools, and then click Disk Cleanup.

2   Make sure that your hard disk drive is displayed in the Drives box, and then click OK.

3   In the Files To Delete list, select the Recycle Bin check box and Temporary Files check box, and then click OK. Click Yes.

To fix hard disk problems before they happen

1   Click the Start button, point to Programs, point to Accessories, point to System Tools, and then click ScanDisk.

2   Select the Automatically Fix Errors check box.

3   Click Start.

4   Click Close to close the ScanDisk results, and then in the ScanDisk dialog box, click Close.

To keep your hard disk running smoothly

1   Click the Start button, point to Programs, point to Accessories, point to System Tools, and then click Disk Defragmenter.

2   Click OK to start Disk Defragmenter, and then click Show Details.

3   In the Defragmenting Drive dialog box, click Legend, and then click Yes.

To schedule tasks

1   Click the Start button, point to Programs, point to Accessories, point to System Tools, and then click Scheduled Tasks.

2   Double-click Add Scheduled Task.

3   Work through the steps in the Scheduled Task Wizard.

To manage power settings

1   Click the Start button, point to Settings, and then click Control Panel.

2   Double-click Power Options, click the Power Scheme down arrow, and then select a power scheme.

3   To create a custom power scheme, select time intervals in the Settings area, click Save As, type a name, and then click OK.

4   To enable a power scheme, click Apply.

7

Backing Up Files and Adding Hardware

After completing this lesson, you will be able to:

ESTIMATED TIME 20 min.

✔ *Back up files to a floppy disk.*

✔ *Restore files that have been backed up.*

✔ *Install a printer and then change the printer settings.*

✔ *Install a network printer to share on your home network.*

For additional information on copying practice files, see the "Using the Microsoft Windows Me Step by Step CD-ROM" section at the beginning of this book.

Now that you are familiar with Microsoft Windows Millennium Edition, there are two additional tasks that you will periodically perform as you continue to use Windows Me: backing up files and installing printers. Backing up files is a task that you need to do frequently and conscientiously—if not, you will lose important files sooner or later. Installing printers is a task that you will do less frequently, but you will probably upgrade your printer or add a second printer, share printers on your home network, and adjust printer settings.

In this lesson, you will learn how to back up and **restore** document files to a floppy disk. You will also learn how to install a printer, change printer properties, and share a printer on your home network.

Practice files for the lesson

To complete the exercises in the lesson, you will need to use the Windows Me SBS folder and the files in the Family Photos folder. Before you can work with any of these exercise files, you must copy the folders from the Microsoft Windows Me Step by Step CD-ROM to your hard disk.

Backing Up Files

Although today's hardware and software are usually reliable, they are not infallibly reliable. Sooner or later you will encounter a problem that will make it difficult or impossible to find and use documents stored on your computer, unless you have backed up the documents. For example, hard disks, although generally reliable, can fail more easily than some other computer components because they contain moving parts that wear as they are used. If your hard disk fails, you can lose all of your documents stored on it. Documents can also be lost because of a software failure or even because you mistakenly delete a document and are unable to recover it. When you back up files, you usually copy them to another medium, such as a floppy disk.

Installing Microsoft Windows Backup

In previous versions of Microsoft Windows, Microsoft Windows Backup was a component that was typically installed during Windows setup. In Microsoft Windows Millennium Edition, Backup is a separate program and must be installed directly from the Windows Me CD-ROM.

If you installed Windows Me over an older version of Windows in which the older version of Backup was already installed, the new Backup will not automatically replace the older version, nor will the older version be removed. You can check to see if the new version of Backup has been installed on your computer. In Control Panel, double-click Add/Remove Programs. If Microsoft Windows Backup is listed in the first tab, then the newest version of Backup has been installed on your computer. If not, complete the following steps to install it.

1   Insert the Microsoft Windows Me CD-ROM in your CD-ROM drive. If the contents of the CD-ROM drive are not displayed, double-click the My Computer icon, and then double-click the CD-ROM drive icon.

2   On the Windows Me CD-ROM screen, click Browse This CD, and then double-click the Add-Ons folder.

3   Double-click the MSBackup folder, and then double-click the Msbexp file to install Backup.

4   When a message indicating that the installation is complete appears, click OK. When you are prompted to restart your computer, click Yes, and then remove the CD-ROM from the CD-ROM drive.

5   Close MSBackup, and then close My Computer.

To be safe, you need to back up your hard disk on a regular basis. If you have extremely important documents, such as financial records that you access every day, you might want to back them up daily. Other documents might be backed up on a less stringent schedule—every other day, weekly, or monthly—based on how often you access them and how difficult they would be to replicate if lost.

Microsoft Windows Millennium Edition includes Microsoft Windows Backup, which is a program that you can use to back up and restore documents on your computer. When you use Backup, you have several options. You can do a full-system **backup**, which backs up all files on your computer, including program files and Windows Me. Or, you can select certain files to be backed up, such as only your document files. When you do subsequent backups, you can choose to back up everything again, or back up only those files that have changed since your first backup.

In addition to deciding what to back up, you also have to consider the medium used for the backup. You can back up your files to your hard disk, but usually that is not the best choice, since you usually back up files to protect yourself against hard disk failure. You can back up your files to a floppy disk, but you have limited space, requiring you to use quite a few disks. However, backing up your files to a floppy disk might be a good choice when you are only backing up one file.

You can also back up your files to other removable media, such as Iomega Zip drives, which provide much more storage space (typically 100 MB or 200 MB) than a floppy disk. You can also back up your files to a tape or to another hard disk, even to the hard disk of another computer on your home network. The medium you choose might require special hardware, such as a Zip or tape drive. Check with your computer documentation or manufacturer to see what media is supported by your computer.

Once you choose how often you want to back up your files, an efficient strategy is to back up document files only. If your hard disk fails, you can reinstall the software from the original software disks. Once you have backed up all of your document files, you can do incremental backups, which means that you back up only new and changed files during subsequent backups, saving both time and space because fewer files will usually need to be backed up.

tip

Make a careful inventory of the files you want to back up so that you do not inadvertently miss including critical files. Some programs, such as money-management programs like Microsoft Money, might store data files in a default directory that is easy to overlook. You should also consider backing up your Inbox and Address Book, because information they contain can be difficult to replace.

7

Backing Up Files

In this exercise, you are concerned about safeguarding the document files on your computer. You want to try Backup before deciding on a schedule and selecting the data files you want to include in your backups. As a test, you decide to back up the files in your Family Photos folder to a floppy disk.

You can also start the Backup Wizard from the Microsoft Backup dialog box. On the Standard toolbar, click the Backup Wizard button.

Backup Wizard

1   Click the Start button, point to Programs, point to Accessories, point to System Tools, and then click Backup.

If you have no backup devices, such as a tape drive, attached to your system, a message indicating that no backup devices were found on your computer will appear.

> ## tip
> If you do have a backup device installed that Backup has not detected, click Yes. The Add New Hardware Wizard starts, and Windows Me will search for the device.

For a demonstration of how to back up files, in the Multimedia folder on the Microsoft Windows Me Step by Step CD-ROM, double-click BackingUpFiles.

2   If you do not have a backup device installed, click No.

The Microsoft Backup dialog box appears.

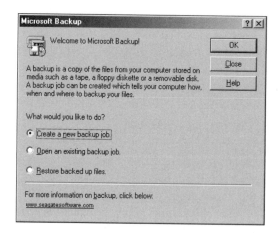

3   Make sure that Create A New Backup Job is selected, and then click OK.

To back up the entire contents of your hard disk, click the Back Up My Computer option.

4   Click the Back Up Selected Files, Folders, And Drives option, and then click Next to select the folders and files you want to back up.

5   Click the plus sign (+) next to drive C, click the plus sign next to the Windows Me SBS folder, and then select the Family Photos check box to back up the contents of the Family Photos folder.

important

You can double-click the folder to view the folder contents.

When you select a folder check box, all of the individual files in the folder as well as all subfolders are also selected and will be backed up. If you want to back up individual files, double-click the folder to view the folder contents, and then select the files you want to back up.

6   Click Next, and then make sure that All Selected Files is selected.

tip

Once you have initially backed up your files and are doing subsequent back-ups of the same folder, you can select New And Changed Files on the What To Back Up screen. Only files that have been changed since your previous backup session will be backed up.

7   Click Next.

The Where To Back Up Screen appears. By default, the selected files are backed up to C:\MyBackup.

Up One Level

8   Insert a floppy disk in your floppy drive, click the folder button next to the C:\:MyBackup box, click the Up One Level button, and then double-click the floppy disk icon.

tip

It's always a good idea to write the name and date of the backup on the backup medium. If you need to restore the files later, you will know which medium to use.

9   In the File Name box, type **Family Photos** click Open, and then click Next.

10   Make sure that the Compare Original And Backup Files To Verify Data Was Successfully Backed Up check box and the Compress The Backup Data To Save Space check box are selected.

Backup files use a special format designated by the file extension .qic.

Backup will verify that your files were correctly backed up and compress your files to save space.

11   Click Next, and then in the Type A Name For This Backup Job box, type **Personal Files**

The Name The Backup Job screen summarizes the backup settings.

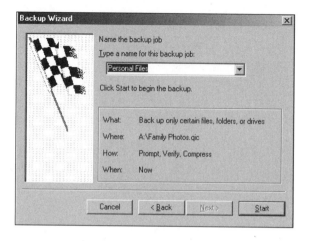

To change the backup settings, click Back to locate the wizard screen where you want to make changes.

12   Click Start.

As the backup process starts, the Backup Progress dialog box appears, which lists the backup settings and tracks the progress of the backup. When the backup is complete, a message indicating that the backup is complete is displayed. Note that the file you backed up was compressed during the backup operation.

13   Click OK, and then click Report.

A report describing the backup job is displayed.

14   In the Backup Report window, click Close, click OK, and then in the Microsoft Backup dialog box, click Close.

tip

You can back up files without using the Backup Wizard by entering settings directly in the Backup tab of the Microsoft Windows Backup dialog box. You can also set backup options by clicking Options in the Backup dialog box and set preferences by clicking Preferences on the Tools menu. For more information on backup options and preferences, see Backup Help.

Restoring Files

To restore files means to copy the backup versions of the files to another location where they can be used. Usually the files are restored to their original location. When you restore files using Backup, you can use the Restore Wizard, which steps you through the process of selecting restore options, such as selecting the files you want to restore and identifying the location where to restore them. Once you have selected the required options, Backup restores the files, and you can use them just as if they were the originals.

In this exercise, now that you have practiced backing up a folder, you want to try out the restore process. To make the process more realistic, you decide first to move the existing Family Photos folder to My Documents. By moving the Family Photos folder, you are simulating a disaster in which the folder has been accidentally deleted from your hard disk. You will also be able to inspect the restored files and compare them to the originals.

You can also start the Restore Wizard from the Backup dialog box. On the Standard toolbar, click the Restore Wizard button.

Restore Wizard

1   Double-click the My Computer icon, double-click the Local Disk icon, and then double-click the Windows Me SBS folder.

2   On the Standard toolbar, click Folders, and then drag the Family Photos folder to the My Documents folder. Then, minimize the Windows Me SBS folder.

3   Make sure that the disk containing the backed up files is in the floppy drive. Click the Start button, point to Programs, point to Accessories, point to System Tools, and then click Backup.

A message welcoming you to Microsoft Backup is displayed.

4   Click Restore Backed Up Files, and then click OK.

The Restore Wizard starts.

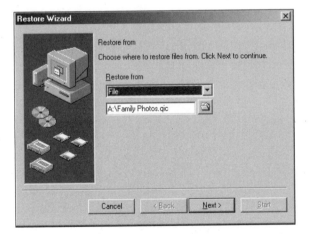

tip
If you have created more than one backup file, you can choose the file you want to restore from the second Restore From box.

5   Make sure that the location and file name of your backed up files are displayed in the second Restore From box, and then click Next.

The Select Backup Sets dialog box appears, listing the Personal Files backup file.

6   Make sure that the Personal Files backup is selected, and click OK.

A message appears briefly, indicating that Backup is logging the operation, and then the Restore Wizard appears again.

7   In the What To Restore list, expand the hard disk, expand the Windows Me SBS folder, select the Family Photos check box, and then click Next.

The Where To Restore screen appears.

tip

To choose an alternate location, click the arrow in the Where To Restore box, click Alternate Location, click the folder icon, and then select an alternate location.

8   In the Where To Restore box, make sure that Original Location is selected, and then click Next.

The How To Restore screen appears.

9   Make sure that Do Not Replace The File On My Computer (Recommended) is selected, and then click Start.

A message explaining that the listed media is required is displayed.

tip

The Do Not Replace The File On My Computer option is recommended so that you do not inadvertently replace a file that you have added to or changed but has not been backed up. If you are replacing a file that has been corrupted and is still on your computer, you should choose one of the other two options to replace the corrupted file with the backed-up version.

10   Click OK.

The Restore Progress dialog box appears. Once the restore operation has been completed, a message indicating that the operation is completed is displayed.

11 Click OK twice, and then close Backup.

To verify that the restore worked, you can compare the files in the restored folder with the files in the folder you moved to My Documents.

12 Open the Windows Me SBS folder.

The Family Photos folder has been restored to the Windows Me SBS folder.

13 Close the Windows Me SBS folder.

tip

You can restore files without using the Restore Wizard by entering settings directly in the Microsoft Backup dialog box. You can also set restore options by clicking the Restore tab in the Backup dialog box. Click Options to change restore options and set preferences by clicking Preferences on the Tools menu. For more information on backup options and preferences, see Backup Help.

Reviewing System Settings

If you want to learn more about your computer and how it is set up, you can see a general overview of your computer system and the hardware devices attached to it. The information can be especially helpful if you have to troubleshoot a device that isn't working correctly. The System Properties dialog box provides an overview of your system and the hardware attached to it.

To view System Properties, right-click the My Computer icon and then click Properties. You can also double-click the System icon in Control Panel.

Although you can change some of the hardware settings from System Properties, you probably won't want to unless you are a more advanced user or are very adventurous. Indeed, changing device settings without knowing what you are doing can cause unexpected and sometimes disastrous consequences.

On the other hand, System Properties is the most convenient place to find basic information about how your computer is set up. In addition, if you ever have trouble with your computer or software and call a support technician for help, you might be asked to check device settings in System Resources.

(continued)

7

Backing Up Files

continued

Help

To find out specific information about items in the Systems Resources dialog box, go to a specific tab, click the Help button on the title bar, and then click the item you want to know about. In Systems Properties you can find:

■ General information about your system. The General tab in the System Properties dialog box lists the particular version of Windows that you are using, your computer name and serial number, and the type of **processor** and amount of **RAM** in your system.

■ Information about hardware devices. The Device Manager tab lists hardware devices attached to your computer and their properties. For example, if you expand the Hard Disk Controller item, select your hard disk, and then click Properties, you will see information about the device that controls how your hard disk operates. If a device has been disabled, you will see an X on the icon next to the device. A circled exclamation point indicates that the device has a problem. You can usually find out more by viewing the properties for that device.

■ Information about hardware profiles set up on your computer. Hardware profiles tell the computer which device **drivers** to load. Some computers might have more than one profile—for example, laptops that can be attached to a **docking station**.

■ Current system performance information. You can view information about your computer's memory and how much of your system resources are being used at the moment.

Installing a Printer and Changing Printer Settings

To install a network printer, see the following section, "Sharing Printers on Your Home Network."

Newer printers often come with installation software, which you use much like software that installs a program: you insert the installation disk in a disk drive and then follow the installation instructions to set up the printer.

Microsoft Windows Millennium Edition also includes its own printer setup program that you can use to set up almost any popular printer, including older printers that have long been off the market. The Windows Me installation program can be useful in the following situations:

- The printer software was designed to work with older Microsoft operating systems, such as Windows 3.1 or Windows 95, and not Windows Me.

- You have misplaced your printer installation disk, or you are installing an older printer that does not have an installation disk.

The printer does not have to be physically connected to your computer to add it to Windows.

Once you have installed a printer—using either the Windows Me installation program or the program shipped with the printer—you can view and change printer settings from the Printers folder. The settings you can change depend on the type of printer you have; however, in most cases, you can change the printer port or printer driver you want to use, specify paper size, graphics resolution and color settings, and the default print quality.

In this exercise, you want to set up a printer whose setup disk has been lost. Once you have installed the printer, you want to review the printer settings.

You can also open the Printers folder from Control Panel. In Control Panel, double-click the Printers icon.

1 Click the Start button, point to Settings, and then click Printers.

The Printers folder opens.

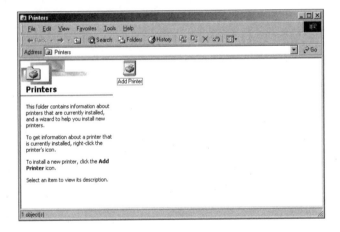

The printer selected here is for demonstration purposes only. Instructions for deleting the printer appear in the Lesson Wrap-Up section of this lesson.

2 Double-click the Add Printer icon to start the Add Printer Wizard, and then click Next.

3 Make sure that Local Printer is selected, and then click Next.

4 In the Manufacturers list, scroll down and click Canon, and then in the Printers list, click Canon Bubble-Jet BJ-30.

> **tip**
>
> Windows Me comes with updated printer drivers for many common printers, so you usually just select the manufacturer and model from the Add Printer Wizard. However, if you have a newer printer driver from the printer manufacturer, you will probably want to use that instead of the driver shipped with Windows. To install the new driver, click Have Disk.

5   Click Next, select LPT1, and then click Next.

The Printer Name screen appears, and Canon Bubble-Jet BJ-30 is displayed in the Printer Name box. If it would help you identify the printer better, you can rename it by typing a new name.

> **tip**
>
> Most computers use the LPT1 printer port for connecting printers. If you do not have an LPT1 port or are unsure which port to choose, consult your computer documentation or contact the computer manufacturer.

If the printer is connected to your computer, Windows recommends that you print a test page.

6   Click Next, click No, and then click Finish.

A message indicating that printer files are being copied to your computer is displayed, and then a printer icon for the printer is added to the Printers folder. A check mark next to the icon indicates that the printer is your default printer. If you have allowed printer sharing on your computer, the new printer icon indicates that it is a shared device.

> **tip**
>
> You can make a printer that you have already set up your default printer. In the Printers folder, right-click the printer icon that you want to make your default printer, and then click Set As Default.

To delete a printer, right-click the printer icon, and then click Delete.

7   Right-click the Canon Bubble-Jet BJ-30 printer icon, and then click Properties to open the Properties dialog box.

Help

tip

You can get help on printer properties by clicking a tab in the Properties dialog box, clicking the Help button on the title bar, and then clicking the item you want help for.

8   Click the Paper tab, and then in the Paper Size area, scroll to the right until the #10 envelope icon appears.

The Canon printer is set to print a standard-size business envelope.

9   In the Canon Bubble-Jet BJ-30 Properties dialog box, click OK to close the Printers folder.

tip

When you print, a printer icon appears on the right side of the taskbar. You can double-click the icon to open the folder for that printer, which will list the document currently printing and any documents queued for printing. You can pause or cancel the printing by right-clicking the document name, and then clicking Pause Printing or Cancel Printing.

Sharing Printers on Your Home Network

For information on setting up a home network, see Lesson 3, "Using a Home Network."

If you have not set up a printer on your computer, see the previous section, "Installing a Printer and Changing Printer Settings."

If you have more than one computer, you will probably want to print files from each computer. You can, of course, purchase a printer for each computer, or you can get by with one printer by copying the files you want to print to a floppy disk, transporting the disk to the computer with the printer, and then printing. Or, an easier and more efficient method is to share one printer on your home network. When you share a printer, you can print from any computer located on your network. In fact, you can share other devices as well, such as scanners or external disk drives.

To share a printer, you need to make sure that the printer is set up on the computer it is attached to. Then, on the same computer, you turn on printer sharing and share the printer, much as you would share a folder. Finally, you set up the other computer to use the printer.

Backing Up Files

7

Shared Printer

important

You do not need to complete this exercise if you installed a home network with a printer already attached to the client computer and shared the printer during the home network setup. If the printer is already shared, the Shared Printer icon will be displayed in the Printers folder.

Your computers will need to be connected to a home network to complete this exercise, and you must have a printer installed on your computer.

In this exercise, your family has one printer, which is attached to your computer running Windows Me and is already set up. You decide to set up printer sharing so that anyone using another computer on the network will be able to print too. You share the printer on your computer running Windows Me and then set up your computer running Windows 98 to print from the shared printer.

1   On your new computer, click the Start button, point to Settings, and then click Control Panel.

2   Double-click the Network icon, and then click File And Print Sharing.

3   Select the I Want To Be Able To Allow Others To Print To My Printer(s) check box, and then click OK twice.

4   When you are prompted to restart your computer, click Yes.

    After your computer restarts, it is set up to share printers.

You can also click the Start button, point to Settings, and then click Printers.

5   In Control Panel, double-click the Printers icon.

    The Printers dialog box appears. An icon for the printer that has been set up on your computer is displayed in the dialog box.

6   Right-click the printer you set up, and then click Sharing.

    The Properties dialog box for your printer appears.

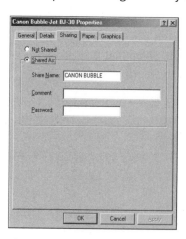

7 Click Shared As, and then click OK.

The printer icon is replaced by the Shared Printer icon.

> **tip**
>
> From the Printer Properties dialog box, you can assign a new name to the shared printer, add a comment, or assign a password to control access to the printer.

8 Close the Printers dialog box, and then close Control Panel.

9 On your other computer, click the Start button, point to Settings, and then click Printers.

The Printers dialog box appears.

10 Double-click the Add Printer icon.

The Add Printer Wizard starts.

> **tip**
>
> If a printer is already set up on your computer, you can also share it when you set up a home network. For more information, see Lesson 3, "Using a Home Network."

11 Click Next.

A message asking how your printer is attached to your computer is displayed.

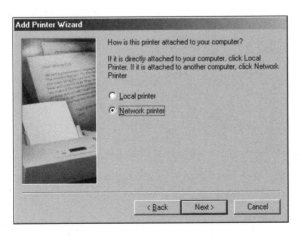

12 Click Network Printer, and then click Next.

You will set up the printer on your home network. A message explaining that you need to type the network path of your printer is displayed.

13 Click Browse.

The Browse For Printer dialog box appears, displaying the contents of your Network Neighborhood.

14 Expand Entire Network, select the printer you want to print to, and then click OK.

The printer path is displayed in the Network Path Or Queue Name box of the Add Printer Wizard.

If you print from MS-DOS-based programs, click Yes under Do You Print From MS-DOS-Based Programs.

15 Click Next, and then under Do You Want Your Windows-Based Programs To Use This Printer As The Default Printer?, click Yes.

Windows programs on this computer will automatically print to the computer you are setting up.

16 Click Next, make sure that No is selected under Would You Like To Print A Test Page?, and then click Finish.

A message indicating that files are being copied is displayed, and then a test page is printed. When you print from a Windows program, it will automatically be sent to the network printer.

Installing Other Hardware

When you add new **Plug and Play** hardware to your computer—for example, a DVD drive, modem, or network adapter—Microsoft Windows Millennium Edition detects the new hardware after you have physically installed it and then updates your system files. All you have to do is turn off your computer, attach the device to your computer, and turn it on again—and the device works. Windows Me does the rest.

Most new devices on the market are Plug and Play, so adding them to Windows Me is usually not a problem. In fact, many devices have their own installation software that includes any necessary drivers you need to run the hardware. If you are using installation software supplied with the device, you usually attach the device first and then run the hardware; it is very important to read your installation instructions first.

If you are installing hardware that is not Plug and Play and does not include its own installation program, you can use the Windows Me Add New Hardware Wizard.

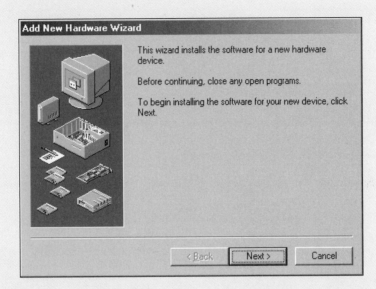

To run the wizard, open Control Panel, and then double-click Add New Hardware. Before you run the wizard, you need to physically install the device. Then, make sure that no other programs are running on your computer when you start the wizard. In addition, if you have a driver for the device, make sure that you have that handy before starting the wizard.

If you do have trouble getting a new device running—Plug and Play or not—you can use the Windows Me Hardware Troubleshooter. The trouble-shooter takes you step by step through discovering and fixing common hardware problems. To locate the troubleshooter, start Windows Me Help, and then type **Hardware** in the Search Help And Support box. Scroll down in the results list to locate "Hardware Troubleshooter."

Finally, if you want to uninstall a device, open the System Properties folder, click the Device Manager tab, right-click the device you want to remove, and then click Remove. For more information on system properties, see "Reviewing System Settings" earlier in this lesson.

Installing a USB Device

Most new computers come with at least one universal serial bus (USB) port, making adding a hardware device as simple as plugging your computer into an electrical outlet.

For more information on serial and parallel ports, see Lesson 3, "Using a Home Network."

A serial bus is a circuit inside your computer that transports data among various components. A USB is a special type of serial bus that is used for connecting hardware to your computer. The USB port is typically located on the back of your computer, along with standard serial and parallel ports, and is a small rectangular port about an inch long.

When you buy a hardware device that is designed to be plugged into a USB port, you can plug the device in while your computer is on and then use the device immediately. You don't have to turn your computer off, and you don't have to install the device. That makes USB ports an easy way to add new hardware, and they are especially useful for hardware devices you might use on several computers, such as game devices or printers. Each time you want to use the device on a different computer, just unplug the device from one computer and plug it into the next. In addition, USB devices usually use power from the computer, so you don't need to also plug them into an electrical outlet.

Another advantage of USB devices is that you can connect up to 127 USB devices to your computer. You can buy a special hardware device that contains additional USB ports to connect to your USB port, much like a power strip that you plug into an electrical outlet. Or you can "daisy chain" some USB devices, which means that you can plug one USB device into another. For example, you could plug in a USB printer to your computer's USB port, plug a USB modem into a USB port on your printer, plug a USB game controller into the USB port on your USB modem, and so on.

Lesson Wrap-Up

In Lesson 7, you learned how to back up and restore files to a floppy disk. You also installed a printer, and then set up a printer to share on a home network.

If you are continuing to the next lesson:

1   Close any open windows before continuing.

2   If you want to delete printers that you installed in this lesson, click the Start button, point to Settings, and then click Printers.

3   Right-click the printer you want to delete, and then click Delete.

4   When a message asking if you want to delete printer files appears, click Yes, and then click OK.

If you are not continuing to other lessons:

1   Follow the steps in the previous section for removing items installed in this lesson.

2   If you are finished using your computer for now, log off Windows.

3   If you will not be using your computer for a long time, shut down Windows.

Glossary

backup A duplicate copy of a file that is created in case the original copy is damaged or lost.

docking station A desktop unit into which you plug, or dock, a laptop. The docking station contains power connections, slots for adapter cards, connections for hardware devices, a full-size keyboard, and mouse. A docking unit turns a laptop into a full-size desktop computer so that you have the convenience of a larger keyboard and other devices.

driver A software program that controls a hardware device, such as a printer or modem.

Plug and Play The ability of a computer to automatically configure itself to work with a hardware device connected to it. A user can "plug" in a device, such as a monitor or printer, and "play" it without having to manually configure the system. Also abbreviated "PnP."

processor The electronic unit that controls a computer. Processors are created on chips, small segments of silicon on which microscopic processor circuits are imprinted. Also called "microprocessors."

RAM Random access memory. Information stored in a computer that is available only when the computer is turned on. RAM can be accessed more quickly than information on a storage device such as a hard disk. When the computer is turned off, the RAM contents are erased.

restore To copy backup files from a backup storage device to their original location or a location of your choice.

USB Universal serial bus. A circuit inside your computer that transports data to and from a hardware device and your computer. USB devices are plugged into USB ports on your computer; you do not have to turn the computer off and then back on again or set up the USB device to make it work.

Quick Reference

To back up files

1   Click the Start button, point to Accessories, point to System Tools, and then click Backup.

2   Click OK. Click the Back Up Selected Files, Folders, And Drives option, and then click Next.

3   Select the files to back up, click Next, make sure that All Selected Files is selected, and then click Next.

4   Enter the backup location and backup file name, click Next twice, type a name for the backup job, and then click Start.

5   After the files are backed up, close Backup.

To restore files

1   Make sure that the disk containing the backed up files is in the disk drive or other backup media is set up. Click the Start button, point to Programs, point to Accessories, point to System Tools, and then click Backup.

2   Click Restore Backed Up Files, click OK, make sure that the location and file name of your backed up files are displayed in the second Restore From box, and then click Next.

3   Make sure that the backup set is selected, and click OK.

4   In the What To Restore list, select the appropriate files or folders, click Next, and then in the Where To Restore box, select a location to restore to, and then click Next.

5   Make sure that Do Not Replace The File On My Computer (Recommended) is selected, click Start, and click OK.

6   Click OK, and then close Backup.

To install a printer and change printer settings

1   Click the Start button, point to Settings, and then click Printers.

2   Double-click the Add Printer icon to start the Add Printer Wizard, make sure that Local Printer is selected, and then click Next.

3   In the Manufacturers list, select a printer, click Next, select a printer port, and then click Next.

4   Click Next, click No, and then click Finish.

5   To change printer properties, right-click the printer icon, and click Properties to open the Properties dialog box.

To share printers on your home network

1   On the computer that has the printer to be shared attached, click the Start button, point to Settings, and then click Control Panel.

2   Double-click the Network icon, and then click the File And Print Sharing button.

3   Select the I Want To Be Able To Allow Others To Print To My Printer(s) check box, and then click OK twice.

4   When prompted to restart your computer, click Yes.

5   In Control Panel, double-click the Printers icon.

6   Right-click the printer, click Sharing, click Shared As, and then click OK.

7   Close the Printers dialog box, and then close Control Panel.

8   On your other computer, click the Start button, point to Settings, and then click Printers.

9   Double-click the Add Printer icon, click Next, Click Network Printer, and then click Next. Select the printer you want to print to, and then click OK.

10   Click Next, and then under Do You Want Your Windows-Based Programs To Use This Printer As The Default Printer?, click Yes.

11   Click Next, make sure that Yes is selected under Would You Like To Print A Test Page?, and then click Finish.

Backing Up Files

PART

3

Review & Practice

ESTIMATED TIME 20 min.

Review & Practice

In this Review & Practice section, you have an opportunity to review how to use Microsoft Windows Update to download recent updates to Microsoft Windows Millennium Edition and then how to restore Windows Me with System Restore. You also review deleting unwanted files and scheduling maintenance tasks. Finally, you review how to back up and restore document files and add a printer.

Scenario

You have already helped your neighbor set up Microsoft Windows Millennium Edition on her computer and helped her use some of the Windows Me features. Now she is interested in learning about some of the Windows maintenance tasks, such as updating Windows and backing up files. In particular, she has asked you to show her how to use the following Windows features:

For additional information on copying practice files, see the "Using the Microsoft Windows Me Step by Step CD-ROM" section at the beginning of this book.

- Microsoft Windows Update
- System Restore
- Disk Cleanup
- Scheduled Task Wizard
- Microsoft Windows Backup
- Restore Wizard
- Add Printer Wizard

 To complete the exercises in this Review & Practice, you will need to use the Windows Me SBS folder and the Amy's Images folder. Before you can work with any of these exercise files, you must copy them from the Microsoft Windows Me Step by Step CD-ROM to your hard disk.

You will also need a blank, formatted floppy disk for Step 5.

Step 1:   Update Windows

1   Click the Start button, click Windows Update, and then connect to the Internet when prompted.

2   Click the Product Updates link, and then select and download a component.

3   Quit your browser, and then disconnect from the Internet.

For more information about	See
Keeping Windows up to date	Lesson 6

Step 2:   Restore Windows to a Previous State

1   Quit any open programs, and then click the Start button, point to Programs, point to Accessories, point to System Tools, and then click System Restore.

2   In the Welcome To System Restore Wizard screen, make sure that the Restore My Computer To An Earlier Time option is selected, and then click Next.

3   Work through the remaining steps in the System Restore Wizard.

For more information about	See
Restoring Windows	Lesson 6

Step 3: Clean Up Your Hard Disk

1   Click the Start button, point to Programs, point to Accessories, point to System Tools, and then click Disk Cleanup.

2   Select the drive you want to clean up. Then, select the files you want to delete from your hard disk, click OK, and then click Yes to delete them.

For more information about	See
Cleaning up your hard disk	Lesson 6

Step 4: Schedule Tasks

1   Click the Start button, point to Programs, point to Accessories, point to System Tools, and then click Scheduled Tasks.

2   Work through the Scheduled Task Wizard. Set up Microsoft Outlook Express to start each time you log on to Windows.

3   Restart your computer, and then log on using your profile.

For more information about	See
Scheduling tasks	Lesson 6

Step 5: Back Up Files

1   Insert a blank, formatted floppy disk in your floppy drive. Click the Start button, point to Programs, point to Accessories, point to System Tools, and then click Backup.

2   Click No if you do not have a backup device installed.

3   Make sure that Create A New Backup Job is selected in the Microsoft Backup dialog box, and then click OK.

4   Work through the steps in the Backup Wizard. Back up the files in the Amy's Images folder, located in the Windows Me SBS folder, to your floppy disk.

5   After backing up the files, quit Microsoft Backup.

For more information about	See
Backing up files	Lesson 7

Step 6:   Restore Files

1   Make sure that the disk containing the backed up files is inserted in your floppy drive. Click the Start button, point to Programs, point to Accessories, point to System Tools, and then click Backup.

2   Click the Restore Backed Up Files option in the Microsoft Backup dialog box, and then click OK.

3   Work through the steps in the Restore Wizard.

4   After restoring the files, quit Microsoft Backup – [Restore].

For more information about	See
Restoring files	Lesson 7

Step 7:   Install a Printer

1   Click the Start button, point to Settings, and then click Printers.

2   Double-click the Add Printer icon, and then work through the steps in the Add Printer Wizard. Install a NEC Colormate PS printer on your computer. Do not make the printer your default printer and do not print a test page.

For more information about	See
Installing a printer and changing printer settings	Lesson 7

If you are planning to do other tasks on your computer

1   Close all open folders.

2   To delete the Microsoft Outlook Express scheduled task, open the Schedule Task folder, right-click Outlook Express, and then click Delete.

3   To delete the printer you installed, open the Printers folder, right-click the NEC Colormate PS printer icon, and then click Delete.

If you are not planning to do other tasks on your computer

1   Undo the changes you made during the Review & Practice by following steps 2 and 3 in the previous section.

2   If you are finished using your computer for now, log off Windows.

3   If you will not be using your computer for a long time, shut down Windows.

Matching
the Exercises

Because Microsoft Windows Millennium Edition has many options that affect the desktop, windows, dialog box options, and the operation of certain functions, your computer might look and act differently from what the exercises in this book show. In addition, your screen might not match the screen illustrations in the book if you do not work through the lessons in order. In general, these variations will not affect your ability to perform the exercises. When a specific Windows Me setting or component is required to complete an exercise, the lesson provides information about preparing the setting or component for use in the exercise.

You can ensure that your results correspond as closely as possible with those shown in the exercises by following the steps in this appendix. It isn't essential that you understand the steps in this appendix as you work through them. All steps and settings in this appendix are explained in the lessons and exercises within this book.

Checking the Mouse Settings

The instructions in this book are written for right-handed mouse use, and they assume that your mouse is set for double-clicking to open folders and files and to start programs. (These are the default settings.) If you are left-handed and want to change the mouse button configuration to the Left-Handed option, you will need to reverse the use of the mouse buttons. That is, you will need to left-click whenever exercises specify right-click and right-click when exercises specify left-click. If you change mouse configuration settings, the settings are changed for all user profiles on your computer. To match the default mouse settings, follow these steps:

1   Click the Start button, point to Settings, and then click Control Panel.

2   In Control Panel, double-click the Mouse icon.

3   On the Buttons tab in the Mouse Properties dialog box, click the Right-Handed option, and then click OK.

4   If you prefer to set your mouse for left-handed use, click Left-Handed.

Displaying or Hiding Toolbars

You can show or hide the toolbar in most windows, including My Computer and My Documents. The toolbar settings can be different for each window that you open. You can display or hide toolbars on your screen as appropriate to match the illustrations in this book.

1   In the window, on the View menu, point to Toolbars.

    When a check mark appears next to a toolbar, the toolbar is displayed; if no check mark appears, the toolbar is hidden.

2   On the Toolbars menu, click a toolbar to display or hide it.

Checking Taskbar and Start Menu Settings

You might find certain Microsoft Windows Millennium features, such as Personalized Menus, distracting while you are completing the exercises in this book. In Lesson 1, you are taught how to turn off Personalized Menus, but if you skip that exercise, you might want to turn off the Personalized Menus for the remainder of the lessons. For best results with the exercises, follow these steps to turn Personalized Menus and other Windows features on or off:

1   Right-click the taskbar, and then on the shortcut menu, click Properties.

2   On the General tab in the Taskbar And Start Menu Properties dialog box, select the Always On Top check box and the Show Clock check box. All other check boxes in this tab should be cleared. Click OK.

3   Right-click the taskbar, and then on the shortcut menu, point to Toolbars.

4   On the shortcut menu, verify that Quick Launch is the only toolbar name with a check mark to the left of it. If another toolbar name has a check mark, click the name to remove the check mark.

5   If necessary, repeat steps 3 and 4 until only the Quick Launch bar is selected.

Changing Window Sizes

If the size of your window is different from that shown in the illustrations in the exercises, you can adjust the window.

1   Position the mouse pointer on any edge or corner of the window until the mouse pointer changes to a double-headed arrow.

2   Drag the edge or corner of the window to make the window smaller or larger.
    You can change the window size horizontally by dragging a side or edge, or vertically by dragging the top or bottom; you can simultaneously change the height and the width of a window by dragging a corner.

Restoring Window Sizes

If a window fills the entire screen and you want to see other parts of the desktop, you can restore the window to its previous size.

1   Click the window to make it the active window.

Restore

2   In the upper-right corner of the maximized window, click the Restore button to restore the window to its previous, smaller size.

Changing Views

If the way files appear in a window are different from the illustrations in this book, you can easily change the window view. The views can be different for each window you open.

■   In the window, on the View menu, click Large Icons.

■   The Large Icons view displays large graphical symbols for the files.

Arranging Icons on the Desktop and in Windows

If your desktop icons are jumbled or in a different order from what you want to see, you can re-arrange them. Special windows such as My Documents or My Network Places have specific ways in which icons can be arranged. For example, in My Documents, you can arrange icons by free space.

1   Right-click a blank area on the desktop or in the window.

2   On the desktop or in the window shortcut menu, point to Arrange Icons, and then click Auto Arrange for the default Windows arrangement.

3   Right-click a blank area on the desktop or in the window again. On the Arrange Icons shortcut menu, click By Name, By Type, By Size, or By Date for other icon arrangements.

4   Double-click the My Computer icon. In the My Computer window, right-click, point to Arrange Icons, and then click By Drive Letter, By Type, By Size, or By Free Space for other icon arrangements.

5   To view arrangement options in other windows, view the commands on the Arrange Icons shortcut menu for the specific window.

B

Installing Microsoft Windows Me

This appendix presents information on installing Microsoft Windows Millennium Edition. If you have purchased a new computer, Microsoft Windows Me might have been pre-installed on your computer. If not, you will have to install Windows Me to complete the lessons in this book. You can install Windows Me on either a blank hard disk or as an upgrade to a previous version of Windows.

If Windows Me has been pre-installed, you still might have to install additional Windows Me components to complete some of the exercises. If you need help installing additional components, see "Installing Windows Me Components" later in this appendix.

Preparing Your Computer for Windows Me

Before you install Microsoft Windows Millennium Edition, you should make sure that your computer meets the minimum requirements. If you are upgrading your computer, you should back up your document files before upgrading.

Installing Microsoft Windows Me

There are two Microsoft Windows Millennium Edition packages available for purchase. One is a Full Install package that you use if you are installing Windows Me on a blank hard disk. The other is an Upgrade Install package. You use the Upgrade package if you are upgrading your operating system from an earlier version of Windows. You can also use the Full Install package if you are upgrading from an earlier version of Windows. However, you cannot install the Upgrade Install on a newly formatted hard disk.

When you install Windows Me on a blank hard disk, you will be prompted to choose a setup option. Choose the Typical option, and then in the Windows Components screen, select Display The List Of Components So That I Can Choose The Ones I Want To Install. In the Select Components screen, select the following additional items:

- In the Accessories group, select Briefcase.
- In the Communications group, select Dial-Up Server, Direct Cable Connection, and Internet Connection Sharing.
- In the System Tools group, select Compressed Folders.
- Select WebTV for Windows.

If you install Windows Me over an earlier Windows version, Windows will not prompt you for a setup option. You might need to install some of the Windows components needed for the exercises at a later time. See "Installing Windows Me Components" later in this appendix.

To install Windows Me on a formatted hard disk:

1   Make sure that the drivers for your CD-ROM drive are loaded. If you need assistance with installing these drivers, contact your CD-ROM drive manufacturer or your computer manufacturer.

2   Insert your Windows Me CD in the CD-ROM drive of your computer.

3   At the prompt for the hard disk you want to install Windows Me on—for example, C:\>—type the drive letter of your CD-ROM drive, type a colon, type **setup.exe** and then press Enter. For example, type **D:setup.exe** and then press Enter.

4   When a message asking if you want to continue appears, press Enter to Start Microsoft ScanDisk. Once ScanDisk has finished, press X.

5   When the Welcome To Windows Me Setup screen appears, click Next, and then work through the steps of the Setup Wizard. During setup, you will need the product identification number that is listed on the Window Me CD case.

To install Windows Me over an earlier versions of Windows:

1   Close any programs and insert the Windows Millennium Edition CD in your CD-ROM drive.

2   Depending on your computer, the Windows Millennium CD-ROM dialog box should appear. If it does not, and you are running:

   ■   Windows 3.1: In the Program Manager window, click File, click Run, and then type the drive letter of your CD-ROM drive, type a colon, type **\setup.exe** and then press Enter. For example, type **D:\setup.exe** and then press Enter.

   ■   Windows 95 or 98: Double-click the My Computer icon, double-click your CD-ROM drive, and then double-click Setup.

3   When the Windows Me CD-ROM dialog box appears, click Yes.

4   If a message asking if you want to restart your computer appears, click OK.

5   When the Welcome To Windows Me Setup screen appears, click Next, and then work through the steps of the Setup Wizard. During setup, you will need the product identification number that is listed on the Window Me CD case.

Installing Windows Me Components

Depending on the type of setup you perform and the type of hardware on your computer, Microsoft Windows Millennium Edition might not set up all available components.

But once you have set up Windows Me, you can easily add any component that was not included in the original installation. If you discover you need a Windows Me component not installed on your computer, you use the Add/Remove Programs feature to add the component.

1   Click the Start button, point to Settings, and then click Control Panel.

2   Double-click Add/Remove Program Properties, and then in the Add/Remove Properties dialog box, click the Windows Setup tab.

   If a component is already installed, its check box is selected. Some components include subcomponents. For example, the Accessibility component includes two subcomponents, Accessibility Options and Accessibility Tools. If a check box is selected but appears dimmed, the component includes subcomponents, but not all of them have been selected.

3   Select the component that you want to install.

   If the Details button is available, the component contains subcomponents.

4   To view subcomponents, click Details, select the subcomponents that you want to install, and then click OK.

You can view a description of each component and subcomponent in the Description area.

5   Click OK.

Windows installs the components and subcomponents that you have selected. If the component is not stored on your hard disk, you will be prompted to insert your Windows Me CD.

To install Microsoft Backup, you must use the install program on the Microsoft Windows Me CD-ROM. See the section, "Installing Microsoft Windows Backup" in Lesson 7.

Index

A

Catapult, Inc. & Microsoft Press

Microsoft Windows Me Step by Step has been created by the professional trainers and writers at Catapult, Inc., to the exacting standards you've come to expect from Microsoft Press. Together, we are pleased to present this self-paced training guide, which you can use individually or as part of a class.

Catapult, Inc., is a software training company with years of experience. Catapult's exclusive Performance-Based Training system is available in Catapult training centers across North America and at customer sites. Based on the principles of adult learning, Performance-Based Training ensures that students leave the classroom with confidence and the ability to apply skills to real-world scenarios. *Microsoft Windows Me Step by Step* incorporates Catapult's training expertise to ensure that you'll receive the maximum return on your training time. You'll focus on the skills that can increase your productivity the most while working at your own pace and convenience.

Microsoft Press is the book publishing division of Microsoft Corporation. The leading publisher of information about Microsoft products and services, Microsoft Press is dedicated to providing the highest quality computer books and multimedia training and reference tools that make using Microsoft software easier, more enjoyable, and more productive.

MICROSOFT LICENSE AGREEMENT
Book Companion CD

IMPORTANT—READ CAREFULLY: This Microsoft End-User License Agreement ("EULA") is a legal agreement between you (either an individual or an entity) and Microsoft Corporation for the Microsoft product identified above, which includes computer software and may include associated media, printed materials, and "online" or electronic documentation ("SOFTWARE PROD-UCT"). Any component included within the SOFTWARE PRODUCT that is accompanied by a separate End-User License Agreement shall be governed by such agreement and not the terms set forth below. By installing, copying, or otherwise using the SOFTWARE PRODUCT, you agree to be bound by the terms of this EULA. If you do not agree to the terms of this EULA, you are not authorized to install, copy, or otherwise use the SOFTWARE PRODUCT; you may, however, return the SOFTWARE PROD-UCT, along with all printed materials and other items that form a part of the Microsoft product that includes the SOFTWARE PRODUCT, to the place you obtained them for a full refund.

SOFTWARE PRODUCT LICENSE

The SOFTWARE PRODUCT is protected by United States copyright laws and international copyright treaties, as well as other intellectual property laws and treaties. The SOFTWARE PRODUCT is licensed, not sold.

1. **GRANT OF LICENSE.** This EULA grants you the following rights:

   a. **Software Product.** You may install and use one copy of the SOFTWARE PRODUCT on a single computer. The primary user of the computer on which the SOFTWARE PRODUCT is installed may make a second copy for his or her exclusive use on a portable computer.

   b. **Storage/Network Use.** You may also store or install a copy of the SOFTWARE PRODUCT on a storage device, such as a network server, used only to install or run the SOFTWARE PRODUCT on your other computers over an internal network; however, you must acquire and dedicate a license for each separate computer on which the SOFTWARE PRODUCT is installed or run from the storage device. A license for the SOFTWARE PRODUCT may not be shared or used concurrently on different computers.

   c. **License Pak.** If you have acquired this EULA in a Microsoft License Pak, you may make the number of additional copies of the computer software portion of the SOFTWARE PRODUCT authorized on the printed copy of this EULA, and you may use each copy in the manner specified above. You are also entitled to make a corresponding number of secondary copies for portable computer use as specified above.

   d. **Sample Code.** Solely with respect to portions, if any, of the SOFTWARE PRODUCT that are identified within the SOFT-WARE PRODUCT as sample code (the "SAMPLE CODE"):

      i. **Use and Modification.** Microsoft grants you the right to use and modify the source code version of the SAMPLE CODE, *provided* you comply with subsection (d)(iii) below. You may not distribute the SAMPLE CODE, or any modified version of the SAMPLE CODE, in source code form.

      ii. **Redistributable Files.** Provided you comply with subsection (d)(iii) below, Microsoft grants you a nonexclusive, royalty-free right to reproduce and distribute the object code version of the SAMPLE CODE and of any modified SAMPLE CODE, other than SAMPLE CODE, or any modified version thereof, designated as not redistributable in the Readme file that forms a part of the SOFTWARE PRODUCT (the "Non-Redistributable Sample Code"). All SAMPLE CODE other than the Non-Redistributable Sample Code is collectively referred to as the "REDISTRIBUTABLES."

      iii. **Redistribution Requirements.** If you redistribute the REDISTRIBUTABLES, you agree to: (i) distribute the REDISTRIBUTABLES in object code form only in conjunction with and as a part of your software application product; (ii) not use Microsoft's name, logo, or trademarks to market your software application product; (iii) include a valid copyright notice on your software application product; (iv) indemnify, hold harmless, and defend Microsoft from and against any claims or lawsuits, including attorney's fees, that arise or result from the use or distribution of your software application product; and (v) not permit further distribution of the REDISTRIBUTABLES by your end user. Contact Microsoft for the applicable royalties due and other licensing terms for all other uses and/or distribution of the REDISTRIBUTABLES.

2. **DESCRIPTION OF OTHER RIGHTS AND LIMITATIONS.**

   - **Limitations on Reverse Engineering, Decompilation, and Disassembly.** You may not reverse engineer, decompile, or disassemble the SOFTWARE PRODUCT, except and only to the extent that such activity is expressly permitted by applicable law notwithstanding this limitation.

   - **Separation of Components.** The SOFTWARE PRODUCT is licensed as a single product. Its component parts may not be separated for use on more than one computer.

   - **Rental.** You may not rent, lease, or lend the SOFTWARE PRODUCT.

   - **Support Services.** Microsoft may, but is not obligated to, provide you with support services related to the SOFTWARE PRODUCT ("Support Services"). Use of Support Services is governed by the Microsoft policies and programs described in the user manual, in "online" documentation, and/or in other Microsoft-provided materials. Any supplemental software code provided to you as part of the Support Services shall be considered part of the SOFTWARE PRODUCT and subject to the terms and conditions of this EULA. With respect to technical information you provide to Microsoft as part of the Support Services, Microsoft may use such information for its business purposes, including for product support and development. Microsoft will not utilize such technical information in a form that personally identifies you.

- **Software Transfer.** You may permanently transfer all of your rights under this EULA, provided you retain no copies, you transfer all of the SOFTWARE PRODUCT (including all component parts, the media and printed materials, any upgrades, this EULA, and, if applicable, the Certificate of Authenticity), **and** the recipient agrees to the terms of this EULA.

- **Termination.** Without prejudice to any other rights, Microsoft may terminate this EULA if you fail to comply with the terms and conditions of this EULA. In such event, you must destroy all copies of the SOFTWARE PRODUCT and all of its component parts.

3. **COPYRIGHT.** All title and copyrights in and to the SOFTWARE PRODUCT (including but not limited to any images, photographs, animations, video, audio, music, text, SAMPLE CODE, REDISTRIBUTABLES, and "applets" incorporated into the SOFTWARE PRODUCT) and any copies of the SOFTWARE PRODUCT are owned by Microsoft or its suppliers. The SOFTWARE PRODUCT is protected by copyright laws and international treaty provisions. Therefore, you must treat the SOFTWARE PRODUCT like any other copyrighted material **except** that you may install the SOFTWARE PRODUCT on a single computer provided you keep the original solely for backup or archival purposes. You may not copy the printed materials accompanying the SOFTWARE PRODUCT.

4. **U.S. GOVERNMENT RESTRICTED RIGHTS.** The SOFTWARE PRODUCT and documentation are provided with RESTRICTED RIGHTS. Use, duplication, or disclosure by the Government is subject to restrictions as set forth in subparagraph (c)(1)(ii) of the Rights in Technical Data and Computer Software clause at DFARS 252.227-7013 or subparagraphs (c)(1) and (2) of the Commercial Computer Software—Restricted Rights at 48 CFR 52.227-19, as applicable. Manufacturer is Microsoft Corporation/One Microsoft Way/Redmond, WA 98052-6399.

5. **EXPORT RESTRICTIONS.** You agree that you will not export or re-export the SOFTWARE PRODUCT, any part thereof, or any process or service that is the direct product of the SOFTWARE PRODUCT (the foregoing collectively referred to as the "Restricted Components"), to any country, person, entity, or end user subject to U.S. export restrictions. You specifically agree not to export or re-export any of the Restricted Components (i) to any country to which the U.S. has embargoed or restricted the export of goods or services, which currently include, but are not necessarily limited to, Cuba, Iran, Iraq, Libya, North Korea, Sudan, and Syria, or to any national of any such country, wherever located, who intends to transmit or transport the Restricted Components back to such country; (ii) to any end user who you know or have reason to know will utilize the Restricted Components in the design, development, or production of nuclear, chemical, or biological weapons; or (iii) to any end user who has been prohibited from participating in U.S. export transactions by any federal agency of the U.S. government. You warrant and represent that neither the BXA nor any other U.S. federal agency has suspended, revoked, or denied your export privileges.

DISCLAIMER OF WARRANTY

NO WARRANTIES OR CONDITIONS. MICROSOFT EXPRESSLY DISCLAIMS ANY WARRANTY OR CONDITION FOR THE SOFTWARE PRODUCT. THE SOFTWARE PRODUCT AND ANY RELATED DOCUMENTATION ARE PROVIDED "AS IS" WITHOUT WARRANTY OR CONDITION OF ANY KIND, EITHER EXPRESS OR IMPLIED, INCLUDING, WITHOUT LIMITATION, THE IMPLIED WARRANTIES OF MERCHANTABILITY, FITNESS FOR A PARTICULAR PURPOSE, OR NONINFRINGEMENT. THE ENTIRE RISK ARISING OUT OF USE OR PERFORMANCE OF THE SOFTWARE PRODUCT REMAINS WITH YOU.

LIMITATION OF LIABILITY. TO THE MAXIMUM EXTENT PERMITTED BY APPLICABLE LAW, IN NO EVENT SHALL MICROSOFT OR ITS SUPPLIERS BE LIABLE FOR ANY SPECIAL, INCIDENTAL, INDIRECT, OR CONSEQUENTIAL DAMAGES WHATSOEVER (INCLUDING, WITHOUT LIMITATION, DAMAGES FOR LOSS OF BUSINESS PROFITS, BUSINESS INTERRUPTION, LOSS OF BUSINESS INFORMATION, OR ANY OTHER PECUNIARY LOSS) ARISING OUT OF THE USE OF OR INABILITY TO USE THE SOFTWARE PRODUCT OR THE PROVISION OF OR FAILURE TO PROVIDE SUPPORT SERVICES, EVEN IF MICROSOFT HAS BEEN ADVISED OF THE POSSIBILITY OF SUCH DAMAGES. IN ANY CASE, MICROSOFT'S ENTIRE LIABILITY UNDER ANY PROVISION OF THIS EULA SHALL BE LIMITED TO THE GREATER OF THE AMOUNT ACTUALLY PAID BY YOU FOR THE SOFTWARE PRODUCT OR US$5.00; PROVIDED, HOWEVER, IF YOU HAVE ENTERED INTO A MICROSOFT SUPPORT SERVICES AGREEMENT, MICROSOFT'S ENTIRE LIABILITY REGARDING SUPPORT SERVICES SHALL BE GOVERNED BY THE TERMS OF THAT AGREEMENT. BECAUSE SOME STATES AND JURISDICTIONS DO NOT ALLOW THE EXCLUSION OR LIMITATION OF LIABILITY, THE ABOVE LIMITATION MAY NOT APPLY TO YOU.

MISCELLANEOUS

This EULA is governed by the laws of the State of Washington USA, except and only to the extent that applicable law mandates governing law of a different jurisdiction.

Should you have any questions concerning this EULA, or if you desire to contact Microsoft for any reason, please contact the Microsoft subsidiary serving your country, or write: Microsoft Sales Information Center/One Microsoft Way/Redmond, WA 98052-6399.

The
Microsoft®
Windows Me
Step by Step CD-ROM

The enclosed CD-ROM contains timesaving, ready-to-use practice files that complement the lessons in this book as well as a demonstration of the Microsoft Windows Me Starts Here interactive training product. To use the CD-ROM, you'll need the Microsoft Windows Me operating system.

Before you begin the Step by Step lessons, read the "Using the Microsoft Windows Me Step by Step CD-ROM" section of this book. There you'll find detailed information about the contents of the CD-ROM and easy instructions about how to copy the files to your computer's hard disk.

Please take a few moments to read the License Agreement on the previous page before using the enclosed CD-ROM.

For information about Microsoft Press® products, visit our Web site at

mspress.microsoft.com

Microsoft®